THE POWER OF Joy

Embrace joy and transform your life

Marcia Fry-Galbraith

The Power of Joy: Embrace Joy and Transform Your Life
Published by Three Branches Press
MarciaFryGalbraith.com

ISBN: 979-8-218-65923-3 (paperback)

SELF-HELP / General

THREE BRANCHES
PRESS

CONTENTS

ACKNOWLEDGMENTS

This book is dedicated to my mother and father, who instilled in me the strong foundation that allowed me to believe in myself and to follow my dreams.

To my children, who are always supportive of me and love me through challenges and celebrations. Your love is unwavering. You are my strongest *why* in my journey of life. Thank you for being you and believing in your mom. I love you deeply.

To my inspiring grandchildren, who—when I look into your eyes—are the windows to a bright future filled with love and pure joy. Your Nana loves you unconditionally.

To my friends, who listen patiently, are supportive, and keep me humbled.

To the many patients who have had raw and vulnerable conversations with me behind closed doors that ignited me to write this book.

Special thank you to Besa for always being there for me. You bring out the best in me. Thank you for listening, believing in me and guiding me to my north star.

To my readers—you deserve to have a life overflowing with joy.

FOREWORD

Dear Reader,

I f you are like me, you are a student in this lifetime. By picking up this book, you've already begun the journey. As a student of life, I've been navigating its ups and downs, seeking meaning, purpose, and yes—joy. Like many, I've faced struggles and hardships that often overshadowed my happiness and joy.

I didn't believe that joy is something within my control. For the longest time, I failed to grasp this fundamental truth. I believed that every external circumstance and every person in my life had to change for me to truly experience joy. It was only when my pain became tangible, suffocating, that I realized the need for internal transformation. This book, had it been in my hands at the right time, would have served as a guiding light, illuminating the path from within.

Marcia served women and men in intimate OB-GYN settings where they were present, vulnerable, and being real. With over two decades of experience, Marcia has witnessed the raw vulnerability that emerges in these moments. Despite the incredible progress we've made as a society, Marcia recognizes that many individuals are still missing the joy they deserve. Her message is simple but powerful: The life you want is within your reach, but it begins with a choice—your choice. This book offers a clear map for how to make that choice, how to step into your power, and how to invite joy back into your life.

Marcia's book resonates with me because it empowers individuals to reclaim and maintain joy. She emphasizes boldness in embracing joy, explaining how it can transform lives and empower people to not only change their lives but also influence future generations.

If you do not choose joy for your life, no one else will do it for you. Marcia's diverse and varied approach shares the multitude of choices available to us. Every path begins with a single moment of choosing to step up for yourself, to lead with determination, and to create joy in your life.

I have eagerly awaited Marcia's book since she first shared her passion for supporting men and women and the potential impact of this book. This is Marcia's second book. Her expertise is in developing the best version of yourself. Having appeared on television with Joan Lunden from *Good Morning America* and on numerous radio shows, and shared leadership panels with icons like Stephen Covey and Tony Robbins, Marcia's impact is far-reaching. This book is a testament to her dedication to and belief in the transformative power of joy.

Whether you're just beginning your journey or looking to deepen your sense of fulfillment, this guide is for you. Marcia's insights will inspire you to take charge of your joy and live a life that exceeds your wildest dreams.

I am excited for you, dear reader. You are about to experience the life-changing power of joy.

With anticipation and excitement,
Besa Martini
Life Coach and Business Result Trainer
Robbins Research International

THE QUEST FOR JOY

When was the last time you felt true joy in your life? Do you feel like you spend most of your days running in circles just trying to get everything done? Seldom do we take the time to stop and reflect about our purpose and direction in this short, beautiful life, let alone approach each day with gratitude. We tell ourselves that we don't have time to reflect, yet we all know we need to take the time. We get used to our daily routines. We feel guilty taking much-needed *me time*. I'm not talking about a lot of time, but even ten minutes a day can be life-changing for the quest to find more fulfillment and joy in your life. Do you take the time to enjoy and celebrate your little wins no matter how small they are? There are so many ways to find joy every day in our lives, yet most of us don't embrace the emotion.

Let's start with an important question. Are you where you thought you would be at this stage of your life? Do you ever wake up and look in the mirror and wonder where you are, what you are doing, and how you got there? Do you feel unfulfilled and bored? Do you have the feeling you have more to offer in this beautiful life? For many of us, we have strayed away from our desired journey in life without even realizing it. We find ourselves missing true joy in our lives. Sure, we experience moments of happiness and fun, but I am talking about pure joy. Life does pass so quickly. With a blink of an eye the year has passed, and things haven't changed much. We are all doing basically the same things as we were doing the year before.

One of my niches in life is to help connect the dots of individuals' lives to help them get back on their desired journey, finding their inner joy and purpose. We all have our own *life books*. Our own story is the sum of our past personal experiences and stories that bring us here today. Our thoughts, decisions, and actions control our destiny in life. I look around and see how many of us have lost our joy, our light and happiness in life. I read in a recent study that as of mid-2023, roughly 48 percent of Americans reported feeling depressed or down.[i] So the question is: What has happened to us, and can we rekindle our lives to have more fulfillment? Absolutely! We often find ourselves losing our natural positive outlook on life that we had in childhood. Of course, we all have many life events that can wear us down, but how can we protect the joy we have in life? We often rationalize why we have lost our positive outlooks. We all have so much to be grateful for in our lives. Sometimes we find ourselves pointing to others for our unfulfillment. We blame it on our jobs, our healthcare, our relationships, and the government, just to name a few. We choose to live day by day just trying to get by, not stopping for a moment to see where we are going and how we are actually feeling about our current life. We find ourselves complaining about things that are not happening! We feel numb and apathetic. Do you think that you are where you are today because you chose to follow the path of least resistance for so long and failed to plan your life, making decisions accordingly? Maybe you didn't take the needed time to reflect and reset.

A very important question to ask yourself is: *Do my daily behaviors stack up to what I desire out of life?* You must remember that as we age, our desires change. This is very normal. It's imperative for you to take the time to re-evaluate your decisions and the path you have chosen. The journey of life is an experience of joys, challenges, opportunities, losses, and pain. Self-reflection and reset are crucial for having a fulfilling life filled with joy.

As someone deeply attuned to the emotional landscapes of people's lives, I have noticed a disturbing trend. Many of us have lost our innate sense of joy. Whether it's due to the pressures of work, the strains of personal relationships, or traumas and illnesses, the ability to experience joy seems to be slipping through our hands. This realization has sparked an immense curiosity and a burning desire within me to explore this further, and ultimately to offer a beacon of hope, light, and guidance for you to rekindle the joy in life you truly deserve.

Through my experiences, interactions, and extensive research, I have come to understand that joy is not a fleeting feeling but a lasting state of being that can be reclaimed, nurtured, and sustained. This book aims to be a roadmap for you, offering guidance on how to navigate through life's storms and emerge with a renewed sense of vigor and fulfillment. Writing about joy, especially in such a critical time, is my way of contributing to a better world. It is an invitation to you to look beyond your immediate struggles and to tap into your well of joy that resides within you. By doing so, you will not only enrich your own life but also touch the lives of those around you.

The purpose of this book is multifaceted. It seeks to understand why we lose joy, how we can regain it, and most importantly, how we can sustain it, even in the face of adversity. If you have ever felt that joy is an emotion reserved for the fortunate few, it is my hope that by the end of this book you will realize that you deserve a life full of joy and that it is attainable. I urge you to journal with me through these chapters. Together, we will uncover the truth about joy; it is waiting to be rediscovered by you. My calling is to help you find your joy and lead a healthy life on a daily basis. So, open your heart and curious mind, and let's rekindle our joy together.

You are probably wondering what makes me an expert in this realm. Having worked in the women's healthcare field for over twenty-one years, especially in hands-on medicine in OB-GYN, I was able to hear and share many women's and partners' stories. It was because of my thousands of conversations with patients that I decided to write this book. On the outside, many patients put on a great front that life was great, but in reality the feeling inside wasn't always so sunny.

For so many people, life has no real direction. Just look around and listen to people talking. Many of us allow fear, circumstance, and other people to guide our lives. Have you ever wondered why some people lead exciting lives and for others it's humdrum? Too many of us sit back and depend on someone else to drive our journey and then one day wonder what happened. Many times, our deep reflection occurs when our children leave home, we retire, or we get sick. We got lazy along the way of life.

The good news is that it's never too late to readjust your journey and get back on track. It simply takes goal setting and keeping laser focused with intention, making little changes daily that will lead you to more joy. There is always time to find more joy in your life no matter what age or situation you are currently in. You deserve it.

One day recently, I was having dinner with a close friend. I was telling him that I was not fulfilled with what I have accomplished in life thus far. I was having a pity-me party. He took my hand and said, "You have got to be kidding." I said, "No, I don't feel like I have accomplished enough." He reminded me that I have three accomplished, enlightened children who truly love me, three married-in children who support me in my endeavors, loving grandchildren, and a teaching credential, and that I went to medical school as a physician assistant and practiced for twenty-one years in women's healthcare. I am a life coach and personal coach, had my own medical education company, wrote a book, and spoke all over the United States. I was blessed to have a short spot on *Good Morning America*. I have appeared on public television and many radio talk shows, and the list goes on. I looked at him and started laughing. My response: "I am not done." I have more to accomplish.

I have a saying on my wall, given to me by the same friend, that goes like this: "What do we live for, if it is not to make life less difficult for each other." The quote is from George Eliot. So, I decided to move on to my next step in life—to write this book for you.

I had the opportunity a few years back to attend an Oprah weekend with my best friend. What an experience! It brought to light what this book is all about. There were women in their teens to their nineties. As the light scanned the crowd, I could see women of all ages smiling and dancing. It became very clear that no matter who we are or where we have been, we are all dealing with much of the same stuff. Yes, we are all in different phases of life. We may be more seasoned than others, more highly educated, or more financially secure, but all of us are after joy and fulfillment in life. What is so interesting is that gender, age, color, schooling, and marital status can alter our situations, but in the quietness of the soul, we are all dealing with much of the same stuff on different levels. Oprah was extraordinary in bringing us together to talk about just this! We all need to support one another and spread kindness, joy, and love. The problem is that if one isn't personally fulfilled, it's hard to find joy in one's soul to help others in this world.

So, the big question is: If all of us are looking for more fulfilling lives, then why don't we have them? What I have come to realize is that many of us are in *coast mode*. Many Americans are overweight, do not eat healthily, and do not exercise regularly. Their walk, talk, body, skin, hair, and persona are dull. What the heck? What are we doing with our lives? Those in coast mode seem to be the most unfulfilled in the long run. Depression often sets in. A lot of us question our self-worth. What example and legacy does that set for children or other loved ones around you? You need to dig deep in your soul and rekindle your joy. Trust me, it's there. I realize this is not always easy. But sometimes, we let our grief, trauma and other negative experiences overtake us and we have a hard time breaking through. Does any of this resonate with you? The good news is that you can change your direction in life and be filled with the joy you desire. You have the capacity to turn your thoughts around quickly and experience the life you deserve.

All of us have untapped potential just waiting for us. You must remember, you are the master of your fate and your soul. No one else is going to do it for you—not a parent, not a partner, not a friend. No one else truly understands where you have been or what you have experienced in life. All the past moments of your history stack up to where you are today. Are you ready to take a serious look at yourself, re-evaluate, and make some small changes to help you rekindle more joy in your life? The strongest force in your journey is your ability to define yourself. From there, it's a growth process. That is life: It is a beautiful, humbling gift.

My desire is to help you to think with clarity about what you want in life. I want to help you rekindle your joy and to be for others the light that we all need so much. Let's reset to make your journey more fulfilling for you.

CHAPTER 1

UNDERSTANDING JOY

I define joy as a deep and multifaceted emotion that goes beyond basic pleasure. It encompasses a deep sense of contentment, gratitude, and inner peace that enriches our lives and uplifts our spirits. The concept of joy goes beyond fleeting moments of pleasure or external circumstances. It is a state of being that arises from within, rooted in gratitude, connection, and a deep appreciation for life's beauty and wonder. Let's delve into why joy is so significant for you and how it can transform your life.

The Importance of Joy

Joy empowers you by fostering resilience. So, what is resilience and why is it important for you? According to the American Psychological Association, resilience is "the process and outcome of successfully adapting to difficult or challenging life experiences, especially through mental, emotional, and behavioral flexibility, and adjustment to external and internal demands."[ii] We frequently navigate a multitude of challenges, from managing careers and families to overcoming societal pressures and personal adversities. Joy acts as a buffer for us, enhancing our capacity to bounce back from setbacks and stresses. It provides a reservoir of strength and positivity that helps us face difficulties with grace and poise. By fostering joy, you can navigate the complexities of life with greater ease and perseverance.

Joy nurtures self-love and self-acceptance, which are critical for your healthy self-image. In a world where men and women are scrutinized and held to unrealistic standards, embracing joy can help you cope with these pressures. Joy encourages you to look inward and have appreciation for yourself, fostering a deep sense of self-worth that is not contingent on external validation. This self-acceptance propels you to honor your own needs and desires, leading you to a more authentic and fulfilling life.

I encourage you to take time to look in the mirror on a regular basis, reflect on yourself, and embrace your true self. You can connect with yourself through meditation or taking a walk to think. Regular meditation cultivates a sense of inner peace and contentment, which is a foundation for lasting joy.

Joy also plays a pivotal role in building and maintaining healthy relationships. We often dedicate substantial energy to supporting those around us. However, without a strong foundation of personal joy, this nurturing can become draining. When you experience joy, you are more likely to feel confident and self-assured, which strengthens your ability to set and maintain healthy boundaries. Emotional boundaries are essential for maintaining a healthy sense of self and protecting oneself from emotional harm. Joy enhances your self-worth and self-respect. When we feel good about ourselves, we are less likely to tolerate behavior that compromises our boundaries. Joyful individuals often have more mental and emotional clarity, allowing us to communicate our needs and boundaries more effectively. We can assert what is acceptable and what is not without feeling guilty or anxious. Experiencing joy builds emotional resilience.

Another crucial aspect of joy is its capacity to fuel passion and purpose. Joy is a powerful motivator that forces you to pursue what genuinely excites and inspires you. When you identify and nurture your passions, you will naturally cultivate a purpose-driven life that aligns with your core values and aspirations. This alignment brings a sense of fulfillment and direction, making experiences richer and more meaningful for you.

One of my most favorite things about joy is its ripple effect. It is contagious and inspiring. A joyful individual can impact their surroundings profoundly, uplifting family, friends, and community. Have you ever sat back and watched someone have that effect on others? By prioritizing joy, you not only enrich your own life but also contribute positively to the world around you, creating a cycle of positivity and empowerment. How great is that?

I urge you to take the time to be present and watch the impact you have on others around you when you are feeling joyful. Watch your friends', children's, and coworkers' responses to you. They will be drawn to you because they want to feel the same way! By embracing and cultivating joy, you can unlock your full potential, living a vibrant, empowered, and purpose-driven life.

At its core joy is a state of deep well-being and delight that arises when we align with our true selves, embrace the present moment, and cultivate a sense of gratitude for the blessings in our lives. It is not dependent on external factors or material possessions; rather, joy flows from within, radiating outward and permeating our experiences with a sense of lightness, warmth, and positivity. It is found in the simple pleasures, connections, and moments of beauty that enrich our lives and nourish our souls daily. It's an inner glow that surrounds our being. That's the power of joy. Everyone deserves to have joy in their life, and you can make it happen!

As we begin our journey to explore the concept of joy, remember that joy is not a destination to reach but a way of being. It is a mindset, a choice you make each day to embrace life with an open heart, a curious mind, and a joyful spirit, knowing that true happiness and fulfillment lie in the moments of joy you create, share, and cherish along the way. It's all up to you. Understanding the significance of joy can help you prioritize it in your daily life, leading to a healthier, more satisfying journey. Here are several reasons why joy is important:

Enhances Mental Health

Joy is a powerful remedy for stress, anxiety, and depression. When you experience joy, your brain releases a cocktail of feel-good chemicals, such as endorphins and dopamine, that boost your mood and overall mental health. This positive emotional state can help alleviate the effects of stress and promote a more balanced emotional life. Regular experiences of joy can lead to increased resilience, helping you to better handle life's inevitable challenges.

Improves Physical Health

The benefits of joy also extend to your physical well-being. Joyful experiences can lead to lowered blood pressure, improved immune function, and reduced inflammation. These physiological changes contribute to a longer, healthier life. Additionally, those of us who experience more joy are often more motivated to engage in health-promoting behaviors such as exercise; a healthy, balanced diet; and adequate sleep.

Strengthens Relationships

Joy is contagious and has the power to enhance your social interactions. When you share joyful moments with others, it strengthens your bonds and fosters a sense of community. Positive emotional exchanges build trust and empathy, making your relationships more resilient and supportive. The shared joy in relationships also creates lasting memories, reinforcing your connections with family, friends, and colleagues.

Increases Productivity and Creativity

A joyful state of mind can significantly boost your productivity and creativity. When you feel joyful, your mind is more open to new ideas and solutions, enhancing your problem-solving abilities. This creative flow can lead to innovative thinking and more effective work. Joy also increases your motivation and engagement, making you more effective in your professional and personal endeavors.

Fosters Personal Growth

Joy encourages a positive outlook on life, making you more open to new experiences and opportunities. This openness fosters personal growth and self-improvement. It gives you more mental freedom. When you are joyful, you are more likely to pursue your passions, set and achieve goals, and strive for personal excellence. This continuous growth and development enriches your life and contributes to long-term satisfaction.

Cultivates Gratitude

Experiencing joy often leads to a heightened sense of gratitude. When you take time to recognize and savor joyful moments, you become more aware of the good things in your life. This sense of gratitude can shift your focus from what is lacking to what is abundant, promoting a more positive and content mindset. Gratitude and joy work hand in hand to create a more fulfilling life for you.

Enhances Spiritual Well-Being

For many of us, joy is a deep spiritual experience. It connects you to something greater than yourself and can provide a sense of purpose and meaning. Joyful moments, whether they come from nature, relationships, or personal achievements, often bring to mind a sense of wonder and transcendence. Joy sets a foundation. This spiritual connection can sustain you through difficult times and provide a profound sense of fulfillment.

Acts as a Source of Motivation

Joy can be a significant source of inherent motivation. When you engage in activities that bring you joy, you are driven by an internal desire rather than external pressures. This authentic motivation leads you to more sustainable and enjoyable pursuits. Whether in work, hobbies, or relationships, following your joy can guide you toward a more fulfilling and purpose-driven life. We will talk more about this later in the book.

We all need to support, inspire, and uplift each other as we navigate the twists and turns of our personal evolution, celebrating our victories, learning from our challenges, and embracing the beauty of being fully alive. No, this is not just a dream or a wish but truly a calling for all of us to follow. In the pages that follow, we will explore the principles, practices, and perspectives that can guide you on your path to living your potential, finding the best version of yourself, and discovering joy in your life. Through reflection, intention, and action, you can begin an ever-changing journey of self-discovery, growth, and empowerment that will light up your path and lead you to a life filled with purpose, authenticity, and joy.

As you read, I urge you to take notes. Take time to pause with each section and think about your desired path—your journey. Fill out the action items truthfully, and add pertinent notes after each section so you can reflect on that chapter. Life is full of abundance and blessings that are waiting for you to discover.

ACTION ITEMS

Look in the mirror. What do you see? Write down as many thoughts about how you view yourself as you can in five minutes.

_____

_____

_____

_____

Define what joy looks like in your life.

_____

_____

_____

_____

Write down why you want more joy in your life.

_____

_____

_____

_____

List three to five people you think are leading a life filled with
joy—not celebrities but people in your world.

_____

_____

_____

_____

What are the benefits you are hoping to find when starting on
this journey to fill your life with more joy?

_____

_____

_____

_____

CHAPTER 2

~~~~~~~~~~~~~

WHAT IS HAPPINESS?

When we are thinking about our journey of life, there is a difference between joy and happiness. I want to level set with you in respect to this book, so you have a clear understanding of where I am coming from. I think many of us think of joy and happiness as the same. While the words *joy* and *happiness* are often used interchangeably, they represent two distinct emotional states with different characteristics.

Happiness is a momentary state of mind characterized by feelings of pleasure and satisfaction in response to external events, circumstances, or experiences. It is often due to specific moments of pleasure, success, or fulfillment. Happiness is typically dependent on external factors, such as achievements, relationships, material possessions, or favorable circumstances. It is a reaction to positive events. The problem is that happiness is often short-lived and can vary daily based on changing circumstances. It is a temporary state of emotional well-being that may come and go in response to external stimuli. Happiness is typically more fleeting and situational than joy. It is a surface-level emotion that can fluctuate based on an external event like getting a promotion, receiving a compliment, or enjoying a meal. All of these can induce happiness. While happiness is wonderful, it tends to be temporary and tied to specific outcomes or achievements. Let's delve a little deeper.

One way for us to differentiate between joy and happiness is by considering their triggers. Happiness often results from your positive experiences or material gains. For example, buying a new dress might make you happy, but this feeling usually fades over time. Joy, in contrast, tends to arise from nonmaterial sources like connecting with loved ones, engaging in meaningful work, or practicing gratitude. These sources of joy provide us with a more lasting sense of well-being. Another way to look at this difference is fleeting pleasure versus soul satisfaction.

Moreover, chasing happiness can sometimes lead to a cycle of constantly seeking new experiences or possessions to maintain that state of bliss. This pursuit may cause you stress and dissatisfaction when the anticipated happiness fails to last. On the flip side, cultivating joy involves nurturing a mindset and lifestyle that align with your core values and purpose. This deeper approach fosters a sense of peace and satisfaction that persists even when external circumstances are less than ideal. All of us have had some unfortunate outcomes. Joy is often associated with a sense of wholeness and completeness. Individuals who experience joy are well grounded and connected to something larger than themselves, whether it be nature, spirituality, or community. Happiness, while pleasant, is usually more self-contained and momentary.

Another key distinction lies in our emotional depth. Happiness tends to be a more superficial emotion that's easy to recognize in a smile, laughter, or excitement. Joy, however, can be more profound and subtle. It might manifest as a quiet contentment, a deep sense of peace, or an unshakable resilience in the face of challenges.

Consider this analogy: Happiness is like a burst of fireworks, bright and dazzling but short-lived. Joy is akin to a steady, warm glow from a candle, providing consistent light and warmth over time. Both are valuable, but they serve different purposes in enhancing our lives.

Recently, my six beautiful children, with my close friend, planned a surprise birthday party for me. They planned it perfectly. I was totally surprised when I arrived at the party. There had been so much love put into planning a celebration that involved friends from all different phases of my life. There were people I hadn't seen in years. Clearly, I felt deep joy. I was touched as I went around the room and hugged everyone who came to that special occasion. I will forever cherish that time with my loved ones. When I reflect about that evening, I remember being taken over by pure joy and deep love that I still have today. Sure, I was happy in the moment, but the deep joy of it has not wavered. The effect of that night is like an ever-glowing candle that creates calmness for me. It is a deep feeling of warmth in my heart, knowing the love and sacrifice my friends made for me to attend on that memorable night. On days that are challenging, I often think of that deep joy, and I find a new strength. I am sure you have many of these special moments of joy in your life. It could be a birth, a memorable event, a defining moment with a friend or partner. Savor these moments for a second. Sure, these were happenings that brought on instant happiness, but the effect of joy is much more. The joy has not wavered. These are the moments you want to embrace and hold on to. Remembering these moments can help you through the hard times.

It's important to acknowledge that joy and happiness can coexist and complement each other. We need both of them. Transient moments of happiness can augment an overall sense of joy, and a joyful outlook can make experiences of happiness more meaningful and lasting. In essence, distinguishing between joy and happiness allows you to cultivate a more balanced and fulfilling life. By seeking and nurturing joy, you can develop inner strength and resilience, providing you with a stable foundation to weather life's ups and downs. Meanwhile, embracing moments of happiness can add delightful touches to your everyday experiences.

ACTION ITEMS

Define what happiness is for you.

_____

_____

_____

_____

List five to ten things that make you happy on a daily basis.

_____

_____

_____

_____

List five to ten memories that have brought you everlasting joy in your life.

_____

_____

_____

_____

Write down how you feel when thinking of these special moments.

_____

_____

_____

How can you use these past joyful moments to affect you in your daily life?

_____

_____

_____

_____

CHAPTER 3

～～～✑～～～

ROADBLOCKS TO FINDING JOY

A chieving joy is a personal journey for each one of us. Many of us struggle to find joy in our lives. Here are some things that can prevent you from experiencing joy. Take time now to make notes about what resonates within you.

Feeling Stressed and Overwhelmed

A fast-paced life can steal your joy and dim your light. It puts you at risk of not taking the needed time for self-care and moments of reflection. You need to have quiet time and honor yourself for who you are, where you have been, and what you have. We all need to walk slower and breathe deeper. Every day, take a moment for yourself. In a world filled with challenges, it is crucial to slow down to maintain your inner light—your unique essence, passion, and individuality. This light is not only your driving force but also your gift to the world. Allowing stress or overwhelm to dim your light can hinder your potential and the positive impact you can make.

Negative Thought Patterns

When you start having self-doubt and focusing on all the negative things in your life, you lose sight of your joy. When you focus on the negative, you start a snowball effect. Our emotions control everything. Negative thought patterns can significantly impact your mental and emotional well-being. These patterns often stem from various sources rooted in your past experiences, environmental influences, and biological factors. Understanding where these thoughts originate can empower you to address them and quickly transform them to change your direction. Remember that wherever you focus, your energy will follow.

It is important to understand that one of the primary sources of negative thought patterns is early childhood experiences. During our formative years, we are highly impressionable and rely heavily on our caregivers for emotional guidance. Negative comments, criticism, or lack of support from our parents and authority figures can plant the seeds of self-doubt and insecurity. For instance, if you were consistently told you were not good enough, you may internalize this belief and carry it into adulthood as a negative thought pattern. Take a moment. Can you think of negative feedback given to you in your childhood that has carried into your adulthood? We all have some of these. But just realize that once you understand where the thought is coming from, as it enters your mind, you can change your thoughts to being more positive by viewing them as an opportunity for growth and change. It takes consistent practice, but it's all up to you, as you are the one in control of your thoughts.

Traumatic events such as abuse, loss, death, or illness can also lead you to negative thought patterns. Trauma, at all levels, often leaves emotional scars that manifest as recurrent negative thoughts. These might include feelings of helplessness, fear, or worthlessness. Our brains' response to trauma can create a heightened state of alertness and a tendency for us to focus on potential threats, fostering a negative mindset.

Societal and cultural expectations also play a significant role in feeling joy. Society often imposes unrealistic standards of success, beauty, and behavior, leading you to feel inadequate when you fail to meet these ideals. Media portrayals and social comparisons can exacerbate this, promoting a negative self-image and critical inner dialogue. Negative self-talk—habitually critical inner dialogue—can perpetuate negative thought patterns. Cognitive distortions, such as all-or-nothing thinking, overgeneralization, and catastrophizing, distort reality and reinforce negativity. For example, interpreting a single failure as a universal pattern of incompetence can strengthen a negative mindset. I encourage you to be aware of your thinking and realize that you have the power to flip it to encouraging thoughts.

The environment and your social relationships significantly influence your thought patterns. Being surrounded by negative or toxic individuals can drain your mental energy and reinforce a pessimistic outlook. You know who these people are in your world. They don't make you feel good about life. Sometimes you find yourself more unhappy after being around them. Conversely, having positive and supportive relationships can help replace negative thoughts with more constructive ones. Bottom line: I recommend that you disengage yourself from negative, toxic relationships. I know it's hard; I've been there. But you've got this. They don't serve you. You deserve a life filled with joy and a supportive tribe around you.

Biological factors, including genetics and brain chemistry, cannot be overlooked. Research shows that mental health conditions such as depression and anxiety can influence the prevalence of negative thought patterns.[iii] Neurotransmitters like serotonin and dopamine play crucial roles in mood regulation and imbalances which can lead to persistent negativity and low self-esteem. If you are experiencing depression or anxiety, I encourage you to see a healthcare practitioner. They can help you understand the problem and offer you appropriate treatment. You are not doomed.

Perfectionism and setting unrealistically high expectations for yourself often result in negative thought patterns. The fear of failure and the pressure to meet perfectionist standards can lead to chronic stress, self-criticism, and a constant sense of inadequacy. We all have been around these types of individuals. Many overachievers are perfectionists. A lack of self-compassion also contributes significantly to negative thought patterns. When you are harsh on yourself and lack kindness in your self-assessment, you will foster an internal environment ripe for negativity. Learning self-compassion can counteract these patterns by promoting a more balanced and forgiving inner dialogue.

Finally, a lack of emotional awareness and ineffective coping skills can make it challenging for you to manage your negative thoughts. Those of us who have not developed strategies to process and work through our emotions might find ourselves overwhelmed by negativity, unable to break free from the cycle. Here are some tools and techniques to transform negative thought patterns:

Journaling

Write in your journal, where you can document negative thoughts from the day and the context in which they occurred. Ask yourself probing questions to break down and analyze your negative thoughts. Once you do that, flip them to positive thoughts by saying positive mantras to counteract the negativity. For example, if you hear yourself saying you are not good enough, flip this by saying "I am worthy" three times. This will lead you to a better understanding of yourself and more self-compassion.

Mindfulness and Meditation

Practice mindfulness meditation by being present without judgment. This helps in observing thoughts without getting entangled in them. Download a meditation app on your phone. These apps can be accessed at any time and offer you help on the spot.

Breathing Exercises

Engage in deep breathing techniques to calm your mind and reduce anxiety tied to your negative thoughts. We will discuss some techniques that can help you throughout the day. Take the time to research breath work that feels comfortable for you personally.

Body Scan Meditation

Body scan meditation is a mindfulness exercise that involves focusing on various parts of your body, usually in a sequential manner, to bring awareness and a sense of relaxation. This practice helps you become more present in the moment by paying attention to the physical sensations in each part of your body. It's often used to reduce stress, improve concentration, and enhance overall well-being. During a body scan meditation, you might start with the tips of your toes and gradually move up to the top of your head, noticing without judgment how each part feels. This practice helps cultivate a deeper connection between mind and body, and can be a valuable tool to manage any anxiety and improve your physical and mental health.

As you can see, negative thought patterns stem from a complex interplay of early experiences, trauma, societal influences, biological factors, and personal habits. You can take proactive steps to reframe your thinking and cultivate a more positive and resilient mindset. I urge you to notice your thoughts each day. I know this is a big ask. As you see, feel, or hear negative thoughts enter your mind, push them away. Replace them. Turn them into positive thoughts and empowering statements that you can relate to. I have now come to the point where I put my hand up and push them away as they come into my mind. That works for me. Make it simple.

As you become more attentive to negative thoughts, you will understand how they affect you and hold you back from moving forward positively. Habitual negative thinking, self-criticism, and rumination can create a cycle of pessimism that reinforces a bleak outlook on life. I know many people around me who are constantly talking negatively about life—government, politics, economy, financial costs, inflation, healthcare, and so on. You name it. Just listening to this can exhaust you and suck away your energy. I urge you to be cognizant of it, and when appropriate, walk away gracefully. Leave it behind. It will affect you personally and lower your energy. You are on a mission to have a fulfilling life filled with joy and energy.

Unfulfilling Relationships

I call these empty relationships, and many times toxic relationships. They might be longtime friends that possibly don't serve you anymore. I don't mean to sound cold. But they don't give you the kind of support you need in your current season of life. New friends enter one's life with new seasons. Some people steal our joy because they do not have it themselves. Unfulfilling relationships often harbor negative patterns such as constant criticism, blame, and conflict. Persistent negative interactions can chip away at your self-esteem and mental peace. Criticism and conflict not only cause immediate emotional pain but also contribute to long-term stress and unhappiness. Over time, negative patterns can become ingrained, making it challenging to find joy within yourself. I urge you to let those friends go or set the friendship to the side for a while. Do not look back or feel bad for letting go of toxic relationships. Unfulfilling relationships can have a profound impact on your overall joy and well-being.

One of the primary ways unfulfilling relationships cause a loss of joy is through emotional disconnection. When partners, friends, or family members fail to connect on a deep emotional level, it can lead to feelings of loneliness and isolation. Emotional intimacy is a cornerstone of fulfilling relationships, and its absence can create a void that diminishes joy. The lack of meaningful conversations, empathy, and mutual understanding often leaves you feeling misunderstood and undervalued. When expectations consistently go unmet in a relationship, it leads to disappointment and frustration. Whether you are expecting emotional support during tough times, reciprocation of affection, or simply spending quality time together, unmet expectations can erode the foundation of any

31

relationship. This ongoing disappointment often translates into a chronic sense of dissatisfaction, which diminishes overall joy.

Our supportive relationships provide a safety net during challenging times. Without adequate support, you may feel overwhelmed, stressed, and unable to cope effectively with life's challenges. The absence of a dependable support system makes difficult periods much more burdensome, leading to a decline in overall joy. Try to develop and nourish supportive relationships. I know this might be difficult, but they will help you feel renewed.

Relationships significantly influence our self-worth and identity. In unfulfilling relationships, you may begin to question your value and self-worth. Lack of affirmation and positive reinforcement from a partner or loved one can damage your self-esteem. Incompatibility and misalignment of values, goals, and interests also contribute to unfulfilling relationships. When partners or friends have divergent paths or conflicting values, it can cause tension and disconnection. The struggle to align with someone whose vision of life differs significantly from yours creates stress, overshadowing moments of joy.

Investing time and energy in unfulfilling relationships often means less availability for nurturing fulfilling ones. You can take proactive steps to address these issues. Whether it involves working on communication, seeking support, or re-evaluating the relationship altogether, addressing the root causes can pave the way toward regaining joy and fulfillment in life. I realize it is hard to work on personal relationships, but if they are important to you, take the time and energy needed to make them a priority.

Social Media

In today's digital age, social media has become a major presence in our daily lives. While it offers unparalleled opportunities for connection and sharing, it has a major impact on our emotional well-being, particularly on our sense of joy. It is profound and complex. Despite the promise of social media bringing us closer, many of us find ourselves feeling more isolated and disconnected than ever. Research shows that increased social media usage can lead to feelings of loneliness and decreased life satisfaction.[iv] How can these social platforms designed to connect us leave us feeling so alone? Scrolling through highlight reels of others' lives can lead to constant comparisons, which often diminish our own sense of joy. The pressure to measure up to idealized versions of life portrayed online can foster negative emotions such as envy, inadequacy, and discontent. How does this affect your day-to-day joy?

There is a lot of research being done in this area. A 2025 article in the journal *Body Image* focuses on the impact of social media on body image among young adults.[v] Results show a clear link between social media use—particularly platforms emphasizing visual content—and negative body image perceptions, which can contribute to disorders such as body dysmorphia. Where is the joy in that?

Research published in *Annals of Medicine & Surgery* in 2023 highlights that excessive social media use among adolescents is associated with increased rates of anxiety and depression.[vi] It also notes that continuous exposure to idealized images and lifestyles can contribute to feelings of inadequacy and low self-esteem.

Another great area of concern is the lack of real communication occurring with our increased exposure to social media and lack of in-person social connectivity. There is a lot of research occurring examining how social media influences real-life social interactions. While social media enhances connections and provides a sense of community, it can also diminish the quality of face-to-face interactions, leading to superficial relationships.

I challenge you to take a week to mindfully engage with social media, noticing its effects on your joy and overall well-being. Then, I encourage you to stop all social media use for seven days. Take an inventory of how you are feeling. I bet that at first, you will feel out of the loop or not in touch with your friends and the world. On the other hand, after one week, I think you will start to feel better about your life. While social media has its positives, it can also pose challenges to your mental health and quality of relationships. Understanding and managing its use can help you safeguard your joy.

News

In an era where news is available at our fingertips 24/7, the way we consume information has changed drastically. This constant access to news, while keeping us informed, has significant effects on our emotional well-being and our sense of joy. Research indicates that news coverage is predominantly negative, focusing on disasters, conflicts, and crises. Research is also suggesting that heavy news consumption can lead to a more pessimistic view of the world, often referred to as *mean world syndrome*, which can significantly hamper one's sense of joy and contentment.[vii] Continuous exposure to such content can lead to increased levels of stress, anxiety, and depression. How does this relentless negativity affect your ability to experience joy?

The Psychological Effects

Research suggests that heavy news consumption can distort our perception of reality, making the world seem more dangerous and hostile than it actually is. This heightened sense of threat can erode your senses of security and peace, both of which are critical components of joy.

Emotional Overload

Engaging with emotionally charged news stories can lead to emotional exhaustion. The phenomenon of *compassion fatigue* occurs when constant exposure to others' suffering diminishes our capacity for empathy and joy. How can you manage this emotional overload effectively?

Bias and Joy

News consumption can also reinforce cognitive biases such as negativity bias, where you pay more attention to negative information. This skewed perspective can overshadow positive experiences and diminish your overall sense of joy. How can you counteract these cognitive biases in your daily life?

Behavioral Changes

The way we consume news can also affect our behaviors. For instance, excessive news watching can lead to avoidance behaviors or even addictive patterns, distancing us from activities that nurture joy. A 2022 *Psychology Today* article states that excessive news consumption can lead to changes in mental and physical health and decreased time spent with family and friends.[viii] This behavioral shift can further impact overall emotional well-being and joy. How can you develop healthier news consumption habits?

While it is important to stay informed, it is equally crucial to find a balance that doesn't compromise your joy. Techniques such as mindful consumption, setting limits on news intake, and seeking out positive news can help you preserve your emotional well-being.

Unsatisfying Work

It is incredible how many people today are not satisfied with their jobs. About 77 percent of global employees reported being "not engaged" or "actively disengaged" in their work, according to the 2024 Gallup State of the Global Workplace report.[ix] This statistic indicates that a significant proportion of the workforce is dissatisfied with or not fully invested in their jobs.

The unfortunate side of this is that it is not only affecting these workers but others as well. This dissatisfaction causes a lot of gray clouds in our lives and steals our joy. We typically spend more waking hours at work than we do at home and with our families. Often, problems at work spill over into personal and family life. Once you realize that your dissatisfaction at work is affecting your loved ones and close friends, guilt typically sets in. We find rationales for why we need to remain in our toxic jobs. We feel trapped and unhappy. We are then in a vicious circle of unfulfillment.

I had a job that turned very stressful and unfulfilling to me. All I talked about was how much I didn't like my job. It wore my family and friends out. I wish I had taken steps sooner to leave that job, but I too felt trapped due to my circumstances. I gained so much weight and was sad for way too long. I was losing my natural love of life. I will forever be humbled by my fear of quitting and not moving to a new job. It took a work colleague to convince me that for my own health, the time had come to move on. If you come home daily and complain about what happened at work, it's time to reassess and take action. Here are some actionable steps to increase happiness in the workplace:

Cultivate positive relationships:

- Build strong relationships with colleagues.
- Share appreciation and recognize the efforts of your teammates.
- Engage in team-building activities.

Maintain work-life balance:

- Set clear boundaries between work and personal life.
- Schedule regular breaks throughout the workday.
- Utilize vacation days to recharge.

Create an ergonomic workspace:

- Ensure your workspace is comfortable and conducive to productivity.
- Personalize your desk with items that make you happy and bring you joy.
- Optimize lighting and reduce clutter.

Set clear goals and priorities:

- Break down tasks into manageable steps.
- Use tools like to-do lists or project management apps.
- Focus on one task at a time to avoid feeling overwhelmed.

Seek professional development:

- Pursue opportunities for learning and growth.
- Attend workshops, webinars, or training sessions.
- Set career goals and work toward achieving them.

Practice mindfulness and stress management:

- Incorporate mindfulness exercises such as meditation or deep breathing.
- Take a few minutes each day for a mental reset.
- Manage stress through regular physical activity. Take a walk outside on your lunch break.

Communicate effectively:

- Be open and honest in your communication.
- Listen actively and provide constructive feedback.
- Address conflicts promptly and positively.

Celebrate achievements:

- Recognize and celebrate your own and your team's accomplishments.

- Reward yourself for reaching milestones, no matter how small.

- Keep a positive attitude toward both successes and challenges.

ACTION ITEMS

List your strengths and weaknesses.

_____

_____

_____

_____

What are some negative thoughts you think to yourself repeatedly?

_____

_____

_____

_____

What are the unfulfilling relationships in your life that no longer serve you?

_____

_____

_____

_____

Who are your supporting relationships that you want to spend more time nurturing?

_____

_____

_____

_____

If you are dissatisfied working from home or in the office, list five to ten things you can do to change your situation.

_____

_____

_____

_____

CHAPTER 4

THE UPWARD CLIMB TO
RECLAIMING JOY

It's essential to remember that change is possible. In a moment, you can choose to change your mindset and change your direction—but you have to want it. Knowing *why* you want to change your mindset can help you address underlying issues, seek support, practice self-care, cultivate gratitude, and reframe negative thought patterns. You can gradually shift toward a more positive outlook on life. It's important to acknowledge that finding joy and maintaining a positive mindset is a journey that requires patience, self-compassion, and a willingness to embrace growth and transformation. Remember, you have the power to cultivate joy, resilience, and a cup that overflows with positivity and gratitude.

Start with a strong foundation—recognizing that your light is uniquely yours. It consists of your talents, passions, dreams, and the values that make you who you are. Acknowledge your strengths and the positive attributes that set you apart. This will help reinforce you when you're feeling stressed and overwhelmed. By embracing your uniqueness, you are reinforcing the importance of your inner light. Remember, when you allow someone else to dim your inner light, you are allowing them to suppress your true self. This can lead to feelings of inadequacy, self-doubt, and a decrease in motivation. Understand that your light not only brightens your path but also serves as an example for others. By allowing it to be dimmed, you are depriving yourself and the world of your full potential and the inspiration you can provide.

Change the story you are telling yourself and living, and it will change your direction in life. You will rekindle your joy. The concept of *change your story, change your life* revolves around the idea that the narratives we create about ourselves shape our reality. Here are some pointers:

Become conscious of the stories you tell yourself and others, like "I'm not good enough," or "I always fail." Identifying these narratives is the first step in transforming them. Know that your stories influence your thoughts, emotions, and behaviors. These often limit your potential and happiness. Be watchful and present.

Reframe your narratives from negative to positive. For example, change "I always fail" to "I learn valuable lessons from every experience." It is very important to practice positive self-talk and affirmations to reinforce new, empowering stories.

Visualize your story—imagine yourself succeeding and achieving your goals as part of your new story. See it, breathe it, so you can attain it. Link your new narrative to actionable steps and set achievable goals that align with this positive story. Periodically review and adjust your narratives to ensure you are aligned with your growth and aspirations.

Spend time recognizing and addressing the influences of your childhood so you can better navigate your own journey and contribute positively to the development of future generations. You must stop blaming your childhood for how your life has turned out. Your future is up to you. The first step is to acknowledge your challenges and how they affect you.

Take a moment to write down some of your thoughts about where you are today and any negative feelings about your childhood that have held you back in adulthood. Embrace and recognize them, and list actions you can take to move forward. Blaming your past will put handcuffs on you—take control of your life.

As you become more attentive to negative thoughts, you will understand how they affect you and hold you back. Habitual negative thinking, self-criticism, and rumination can create a cycle of pessimism that reinforces a bleak outlook on life.

You need time to reset and build confidence when dealing with outside pressures. This can be a great time to do the social media fast I mentioned before and connect with people in person. Continue to focus on self-care practices such as proper nutrition, exercise, sleep, and relaxation. These impact your physical and emotional well-being. Without taking care of yourself, it's challenging to cultivate joy and positivity. We will talk more about this extremely important subject.

As human beings, we thrive on connection and belonging, and without meaningful relationships, feeling joy can be difficult. It is important that you find the energy to seek healthy relationships to grow forward in joy and in other areas of your life. A meta-analysis by Julianne Holt-Lunstad and colleagues found that individuals with strong social relationships have a 50 percent increased likelihood of survival compared with those with weaker social ties.[x]

The analysis encompassed data from over three hundred thousand participants across various studies. Researchers at the Harvard T. H. Chan School of Public Health found that having strong social networks and engaging relationships boosts emotional well-being and can decrease the risk of premature death by as much as 33 percent.[xi] These are staggering numbers.

Fine-Tuning Your Purpose and Meaning

Start focusing on your purpose and meaning in life. It might lead your journey on a different path— a path that will be filled with the joy and fulfillment you deserve. How can you find your purpose, connect with what matters to you, and make a difference in the world? We will focus more on purpose later in the book.

Developing Better Coping Skills

Spend time developing your coping mechanisms, improving your stress management, and strengthening your resilience. Without healthy coping strategies, it's easy to feel overwhelmed, defeated, and hopeless. You might wonder if you need better coping skills. Do you experience any of the following?

Avoidance Behavior

Frequently avoiding tasks or situations that cause stress rather than facing them.

Negative Self-Talk

Engaging in persistent negative self-talk or self-blame in challenging situations.

Reliance on Unhealthy Habits

Turning to unhealthy habits such as excessive drinking, overeating, or substance abuse to cope with stress.

Procrastination

Consistently delaying tasks, especially those associated with stress.

Emotional Reactivity

Experiencing frequent mood swings or having difficulty managing emotions during stressful situations.

Withdrawing from Social Networks

Pulling away from friends and family support systems when stressed instead of seeking help or guidance.

Physical Symptoms

Experiencing frequent headaches, body aches, insomnia, or stomach problems when under stress.

Keep present daily. If you see yourself having trouble in any one of the above-mentioned areas, then it's an opportunity for growth.

Positive Affirmations

Practicing positive affirmations can be a rewarding experience. It's a great way to build optimism and self-confidence. So, how do you incorporate these into your life? Start by understanding what you hope to achieve or focus on through positive affirmations. Understanding your personal goals will help tailor your affirmations to be more meaningful and impactful. Create personalized affirmations that resonate with you. These should be stated in the present tense and reflect a positive mindset. For example, if you want to boost self-confidence, an affirmation might be, "I am confident and capable in everything I do." I encourage you to keep the affirmations short and simple. This makes them easier to remember and more likely to be repeated regularly. Consistency is key in making affirmations effective. You can integrate the practice into your daily routine, such as saying them in front of a mirror every morning or before going to bed. Write down these affirmations and place them where you will see them frequently, like on a bathroom mirror or as the wallpaper on your smart phone. I use Post-its and put them where I see them daily. Visualize the affirmation as reality. You can do this! Just remember that long-lasting change takes time. Be patient and give yourself grace.

Gratitude Practices

Gratitude practices can be simple and impactful, offering numerous benefits for emotional well-being and fostering a positive outlook on life. Here are some easy ways to introduce gratitude practices into your daily life. Adopt one or all!

Gratitude Journaling

Keep a gratitude journal where you write down three things you are thankful for each day. This can be done in the morning to set a positive tone for the day or in the evening to reflect on the day's experiences.

Daily Gratitude Moments

Incorporate moments of gratitude into daily routines. For example, before meals, you can pause to appreciate the food and the hands that brought it to your table.

Thank You Notes

Write thank you notes to individuals who have made a difference in your life, whether big or small. This can deepen relationships and reinforce positive feelings. I carry small gratitude cards and leave them with a server or someone who has been kind to me.

Gratitude Meditation

Practice a simple meditation focused on gratitude. This involves sitting quietly and focusing on feelings of thankfulness for specific things or people in your life.

Gratitude Walks

Take walks while reflecting on things you are grateful for. This combines physical movement with mindful appreciation of your surroundings.

Gratitude Jar

Write down things you are thankful for on slips of paper and collect these in a jar. Over time, the jar becomes a visual reminder of the abundance of good in your life.

Modeling Gratitude

Demonstrate gratitude in your own actions and words. When others see gratitude being practiced, they are more likely to adopt the practice themselves.

All these practices can be easily integrated into daily life and provide a positive framework for recognizing and appreciating the good around us.

Behavioral Activation

Schedule activities that bring you joy and accomplishment to counteract negative thoughts. Predict the pleasure you will get from the activities and compare it with actual outcomes.

Self-Compassion

Self-compassion is a wonderful way to help cultivate kindness toward yourself, which can enhance emotional resilience and well-being. Self-compassion involves treating yourself with the same kindness and understanding you would extend to a good friend. It includes recognizing that everyone makes mistakes and experiences difficulties. Be aware of your thoughts and feelings without judgment. This mindfulness helps you become conscious of self-critical patterns and allows for a gentler approach to yourself. Speak to yourself with kindness. You can practice replacing self-critical thoughts with supportive and affirming messages. For instance, instead of "I failed," you can say, "I'm proud of myself for trying." Remember that suffering and imperfection are part of the shared human experience. You are not alone in your struggles. Some people are just better at hiding their problems.

I encourage you to keep practicing self-compassion in your journal, where you can write about moments you found challenging and how you responded to those situations with kindness. When I was raising my children, each night at dinner we would go around the table saying one thing that was negative in our day and how it could have been handled in a positive way. I was trying to teach my children to see the positive, even in challenging moments. Practicing forgiveness toward yourself for past mistakes or perceived failures is important. Each of us is a work in progress.

Take the time to engage in acts of self-care and nurturing activities, such as reading a book, taking a bath, or spending time in nature. The bottom line here is to remember to take self-compassion breaks, where you practice being kind to yourself during stressful moments. Use gestures like placing a hand on your heart to comfort yourself or get a cup of tea. Take a moment of solitude every day at home, work, or even in the car.

Professional Support

Seek professional help such as cognitive behavioral therapy to work through negative thought patterns. Cognitive behavioral therapy is a type of psychotherapy that helps individuals understand and change their thought patterns and behaviors. It's based on the principle that our thoughts, feelings, and behaviors are interconnected, and by changing negative thoughts and behaviors, we can improve our emotional well-being. It helps us identify our negative thoughts, challenge their validity, and replace them with more balanced thoughts. If you find yourself having repeated negative thoughts and behaviors, this may be helpful for you. Consider finding a therapist in your area or online. They can help. Here are some other suggestions to help you with your journey:

Support Groups

Join groups where you can share and gain insights from others experiencing similar struggles.

Counseling

Engage with counselors or life coaches for guidance and support.

Creative Outlets

Use drawing, painting, or other art forms to express and manage your emotions.

Writing

Write in your journal or write stories to process thoughts and feelings creatively.

Music Therapy

Listen to or create music to elevate your mood and shift focus from negative thoughts. This is my go-to. Music clears my mind, helps me think through challenges, and brings me calmness.

Finding Joy While Facing Illness

Finding joy in the face of illness, whether it's yours or a loved one's, can be a deep and overwhelming journey. When illness strikes, it can often feel like your world has been turned upside down. Even in these challenging times, there are ways to find joy and maintain a positive outlook. Here are some suggestions to help you find joy despite facing illness.

First and foremost, it's essential to embrace a mindset of gratitude. Even though illness can bring about numerous hardships, focusing on what you are grateful for can shift your perspective. This might include appreciating small daily pleasures such as a beautiful sunset, the support of loved ones, or simply the comfort of a warm bed. By counting your blessings, you remind yourself that there is still goodness in your life.

Another set of powerful tools is mindfulness and meditation. These practices help anchor you in the present moment, allowing you to fully experience the here and now without being over-whelmed by worries about the future or regrets from the past. The practice of mindfulness reduces stress and improves overall well-being. There are many books and apps that cover mindful-ness. I urge you to delve into this practice, as it can bring much light, joy, inner calmness, and fulfillment.

Connecting with others is critical. Human beings are social creatures, and maintaining strong relationships can provide immense emotional support. Lean on your friends and family or join support groups where you can share your experiences with others who understand what you're going through. These connections can remind you that you are not alone. You can find support groups offering online discussions or video chats that will be a supportive community for you.

Sometimes, illness can prompt a reset of life goals and values. Instead of thinking about all the sadness you are experiencing, use this time to reflect on what truly matters to you. Perhaps you can find joy in helping others, volunteering, or working on a meaningful project if possible. Finding a larger purpose can provide a sense of fulfillment and joy that will aid you through the difficulties of illness.

Laughter truly is one of the best medicines. This is discussed in the well-known book *Anatomy of an Illness as Perceived by the Patient*, by Norman Cousins. Watching a funny movie, reading a humorous book, or simply enjoying the lighthearted company of friends can lift your spirits. Laughter releases endorphins, the body's feel-good chemicals, and can temporarily relieve pain and stress.

Last, self-compassion is crucial. Be kind to yourself during this time. I have spent hours with patients and caregivers helping them see the goodness in their lives as they are being faced with life-threatening illness. Recognize that it's OK to have bad days and to seek help when needed. Treat yourself with the same kindness and patience you would offer a dear friend going through a difficult time. Finding joy in the face of illness may require a concerted effort, but it is entirely possible. By embracing gratitude, mindfulness, creativity, connection, purpose, laughter, and self-compassion, you can nurture your spirit and find moments of joy, even amid the challenges you are facing.

Finding Joy in the Face of Trauma

I have been asked many times if you can find joy after trauma. It is possible to heal and rediscover joy in life by taking intentional steps toward recovery and self-care. These scars must be reckoned with through professional help to grow forward. Past experiences can have strong holds on you. You deserve to come out of the gray clouds and rekindle your joy and happiness. A trained professional such as a physician, counselor, or psychologist can help you find the right person for you.

Remember, you are deserving of love, happiness, and inner peace. You have the strength within you to overcome adversity and rediscover joy in life. Finding joy in the face of dealing with trauma is possible with deliberate effort and a compassionate approach. First, it is crucial to acknowledge and validate your feelings. Trauma can bring a complex array of emotions including sadness, anger, and confusion. Allow yourself to feel these emotions without judgment. Acceptance is the first step toward healing and making space for joy in your life.

Practicing gratitude is another powerful method. Even in the aftermath of trauma, there are still aspects of life that you can cherish and appreciate. By focusing on small, positive experiences such as the kindness of a friend, a comforting meal, or the beauty of nature, you can shift your perspective despite distressing circumstances.

Connecting with others is also essential during this time. Reach out to supportive friends and family, or even support groups. Sharing your experiences and receiving empathy can provide immense comfort. These connections remind you that you are not alone and can offer moments of joy through shared understanding and support.

Engaging in activities that you love will also be a source of joy. Whether it's pursuing a hobby, engaging in physical exercise, or simply spending time in nature, find activities that bring you happiness and make time for them. These moments of joy can act as beacons of light in difficult times.

Mindfulness and meditation are effective tools for coping with trauma. By focusing on the present moment, you can reduce anxiety and prevent your mind from being overwhelmed by past traumas or future worries. Regular mindfulness practice can foster a sense of inner peace and joy. We will talk in more depth about the importance of mindfulness later.

It's important to find deeper meaning and purpose in your experiences. Sometimes, trauma can lead to a reset of your values and goals. Embrace this opportunity to pursue something meaningful that resonates with you, whether that's helping others, learning new skills, or working on a project that ignites your passion. Purpose can be a potent source of joy and fulfillment. Creative activity is another avenue to explore. Art, writing, music, dancing, and other forms of creativity can be incredibly therapeutic. They provide a way to process complex emotions and can serve as a powerful outlet for your feelings. The act of creating something beautiful or meaningful can bring tremendous joy.

Don't underestimate the healing power of humor and laughter. Even amid trauma, finding reasons to laugh can lift your spirits. Watch a funny movie, read a humorous book, or spend time with friends who make you laugh. Laughter releases endorphins and can temporarily reduce pain and stress.

Be gentle with yourself as you navigate through the healing process. Recognize that it's OK to seek help and to have moments of vulnerability. Treat yourself with the same kindness and understanding you would offer a loved one facing trauma. Finding joy in the face of trauma is a journey that requires patience, resilience, and self-compassion. By validating your feelings, embracing gratitude, seeking connections, engaging in joyful activities, practicing mindfulness, finding purpose, expressing creativity, and welcoming laughter, you can nurture your soul and uncover moments of joy despite the hardships.

ACTION ITEMS

Write a paragraph on *why* you want to change your current situation and experience more long-lasting joy in your life.

_____

_____

_____

_____

List three to five negative stories that you hear yourself thinking and or talking about.

_____

_____

_____

_____

Flip each one of those into a positive story. Write them down.

_____

_____

_____

_____

Which coping skills do you want to improve? List ideas of how you are going to change.

_____

_____

_____

_____

List five self-care activities you will do one to two times a week.

_____

_____

_____

_____

List three activities that bring you joy.

_____

_____

_____

_____

Write five to ten positive affirmations on paper and place them strategically at home and at work.

CHAPTER 5

~~~

LIVING TO YOUR FULL POTENTIAL

People around the world face a myriad of challenges that can affect their mental, emotional, and physical well-being. These challenges often stem from societal expectations, workplace dynamics, and personal responsibilities. Despite these hurdles, the intentional cultivation of joy can serve as a powerful tool to transform these difficulties into opportunities for growth and empowerment.

One major challenge many of us encounter is balancing career and family responsibilities. In fact, this is what my first book was about. These challenges can lead us to feelings of overwhelm and burnout. Integrating joy into daily routines, however simple, can make a significant difference. Simple practices such as mindfulness and gratitude rituals can help us stay present and appreciate small moments throughout the day. For instance, taking a few minutes each morning to acknowledge things we are grateful for can shift our mindset from stress to positivity.

Women and other marginalized groups frequently face gender bias and/or inequality in professional settings, which can impact our confidence and career progression. We have come a long way, but we still have a long way to go to be treated equally. What's important is to stay strong and demand to be treated fairly. Be relentless. Celebrating personal achievements, regardless of external validation, can build internal strength and self-assurance. Embracing joy wherever it can be found in these situations can enhance your resilience and foster a sense of self-worth. Encouraging one another to create supportive networks and communities where everyone can share successes and challenges can further amplify the celebration of collective and individual progress.

Another relentless issue is body image and societal pressure to meet certain standards. This pressure often leads us to self-criticism and anxiety, preventing us from experiencing the joy we deserve. Joy can be a revolutionary force by promoting self-acceptance and love for one's unique body. Activities that encourage body positivity, like dancing, yoga, or even mindful walking, can reconnect you with the joy of movement and appreciation for what our bodies are capable of and not just how they look. Moreover, engaging in these joyful physical activities can improve your overall health and well-being. Here are some tips:

- Start small. Begin with short, manageable home workouts, like ten to fifteen minutes of light activity. Start with YouTube, and when you feel less self-conscious, transition to community exercise, as it's important to have support.

- Find a friend to join you for walks or community classes.

- Join a beginner-friendly fitness group or class, which often provides a welcoming environment for a newcomer. Look for local walking clubs or community fitness challenges that aim for inclusivity and support.

- Use music to make your workouts more enjoyable or try dance-based exercises like Zumba.

- Set small, specific goals, such as exercising three times a week, to build consistency without feeling overwhelmed. Make sure the goals work for you but also push you a little.

- Track success and celebrate milestones, no matter how small. These will boost your motivation and confidence.

- Last, don't forget to practice positive affirmations and remind yourself of your progress and commitment whenever you feel self-conscious. It is most important to feel self-confident in your unique body. Beauty comes from the inside out.

Emotional labor and caregiving responsibilities are common additional burdens. Many of us carry these burdens alone and often feel undervalued and exhausted. Joyful activities can provide essential self-care and renewal. Whether accomplished through hobbies, creative pursuits, or simply taking time to relax and unwind, prioritizing joy can replenish your energy and enhance your ability to care for others without neglecting your own needs.

If you are faced with this responsibility, share with a partner or a close friend the desire to have joint responsibilities. This sets up a better world for us and mentors future generations within our family structures.

Navigating big life changes, such as parenting or career transitions, can be challenging. Joy can serve as a stabilizing force during these transitions. Finding joy in new experiences, even amid uncertainty, helps build adaptability and optimism. For example, new parents might find joy in small bonding moments with their baby, while people undergoing career changes might uncover joy in learning new skills and exploring new opportunities. I recommend looking on the web for articles, books, and podcasts that can support you through these challenges.

The power of joy lies in our ability to reframe challenges as opportunities for growth and connection. By intentionally seeking joy, you can transform your approach to life's obstacles, leading to greater resilience, self-esteem, and overall happiness. Joy can help you not only survive but thrive in the face of adversity. The saying "If life gives you lemons, make lemonade" applies here.

Living up to your full potential, finding the best version of yourself, and experiencing joy are essential components of a fulfilling and purposeful life. By embracing personal growth, self-discovery, and a commitment to living authentically, you can unlock your full potential, cultivate your best self, and infuse your life with joy and meaning.

At the core of your potential is the belief that you are capable of greatness, that you possess unique gifts, talents, and strengths waiting to be unleashed. You might not have realized them yet, and that's OK. It is about recognizing your inherent worth, embracing your passions, and pursuing your dreams with courage and determination. When you strive to live up to your full potential, you are not only honoring yourself but also contributing your unique soul and spirit to the world, making a positive impact, and leaving a legacy. This is absolutely within your reach. Finding your best self involves a journey of self-discovery, growth, and transformation. It is about peeling back the layers of conditioning, fears, and limitations to reveal the authentic essence that lies within you. By embracing your true self, acknowledging your values, and aligning your actions with your aspirations, you can step into your power, embody your highest potential, and live a life of purpose, authenticity, fulfillment, and joy.

As you begin on this journey of self-exploration and growth, remember that you are not alone. We all have faced personal struggles, such as health issues, financial difficulties, relationship problems, or mental health challenges. These are a natural part of life. We must get back up and stay in the game. If we withdraw, we are limiting our opportunities for growth. There are many like-minded individuals who are also on a quest to live their full potential, find the best version of themselves, and experience joy in their lives. Seek them out. You might meet them when you least expect it. Together, you can support, inspire, and uplift each other as you navigate the twists and turns of your personal evolution, celebrating your victories, learning from your challenges, and embracing the beauty of being fully alive. Surround yourself with like-minded people wanting more out of life, just like you. Look for groups in your community that have interests similar to yours, like fitness, yoga, Pilates, book club, and so on. At times you might find yourself alone, but stand strong and keep your eye on your north star.

Remember, you must embrace challenges as opportunities for growth, learning, and change. You need to dig deep into your soul and remember who you are, and that you have the strength and perseverance to overcome life's hardships. You will come out stronger and wiser on the other side. Change in life is inevitable. All you need to do to change your journey is change your patterns of thinking. Be patient and kind to yourself while you figure out what brings you joy. Embrace any moment when you feel joy and celebrate it. By focusing on living your full potential, be on the lookout for any challenges, as they may take you on a detour. Deal with them quickly and do your best to compartmentalize them. Move on and don't look back. Remember my friend, your past does not predict your future. There is a future you have not met yet, and it is waiting for you.

ACTION ITEMS

List any challenges you are having at home or work.

_____

_____

_____

_____

Reframe each challenge listed as an opportunity.

_____

_____

_____

_____

Be honest: Are you 100 percent accepting of your unique body? If not, list five things you can do to improve your self-acceptance.

_____

_____

_____

_____

Write down the names of three like-minded friends or family
members that you trust and can be vulnerable with.

_____

_____

_____

_____

CHAPTER 6

FINDING PURPOSE AND PASSION

In the quest for a fulfilling and meaningful life, few endeavors are as important as discovering one's purpose and passion. For many of us, it's a lifetime exploration. Understanding what genuinely drives and inspires you can greatly enhance your quality of life, provide motivation, and contribute to your overall happiness, joy, and sense of fulfillment. Finding your purpose is a profound and life-changing journey that involves self-exploration, reflection, and alignment with your values, passions, and aspirations. It is a process of uncovering your unique gifts, talents, and contributions that you, like everyone, bring to the world. It is about finding meaning and fulfillment in your work at home, in the workplace, and in the community. A strong purpose will help you work through the challenges ahead. Spend time and effort doing only things that align with your philosophy of life. You will find joy in spending your time on the types of activities that will enrich your life and bring you fulfillment. Giving back and serving others in any capacity will give you purpose and joy.

Defining Purpose and Passion

Purpose refers to the fundamental reason for your existence. It is the overarching goal or mission that gives your life direction. It is the belief that your life has meaning and that you have a specific role to play in this world. Passion, on the other hand, is about the activities, subjects, or causes that evoke a deep sense of enthusiasm and joy. Passions are often what you love to do and what you are naturally drawn toward. They bring you energy and satisfaction. While purpose gives you a sense of direction, passion fuels the pursuit of that purpose, making your journey enjoyable and engaging.

The Importance of Finding Your Purpose and Passion

When you are aligned with your purpose and passion, you wake up each day with a sense of excitement and motivation. Your activities feel more meaningful, and you are more likely to be persistent and dedicated, because you are doing what you love and believe in. A clear sense of purpose can drastically improve your mental health by providing a sense of stability and focus. It helps you reduce feelings of aimlessness and depression. Engaging in activities you are passionate about can elevate your mood and provide joy and emotional fulfillment.

Knowing your purpose and having passion can help you endure challenging times. They provide a source of strength and resilience, enabling you to face obstacles with a positive and determined mindset. When you are connected to your purpose, setbacks are seen as temporary hurdles rather than insurmountable barriers. Remember, it is at these times you will grow the most. By aligning yourself with your purpose and passion, you are fostering continuous personal growth. You are more likely to seek out opportunities for learning and self-improvement. This journey of growth and discovery further enriches your life and brings a deep sense of joy and fulfillment. Often, one's purpose is linked to making a positive impact on others or contributing to the greater good. When you live with purpose and passion, you not only enhance your own life but also contribute to the well-being of those around you, creating a ripple effect of positive change and joy.

Steps to Discovering Your Purpose and Passion

Spend time reflecting on your life experiences, interests, and values. Consider what activities make you lose track of time, what subjects you are naturally curious about, and what moments have brought you the most fulfillment. Identify moments when you are so engrossed that hours seem like minutes. These are often indicators of activities you're passionate about. What did you love doing as a child? Revisit childhood memories to uncover hobbies or interests that might still resonate with you today. What topics or issues energize you? Pay attention to subjects or causes that spark excitement or strong emotions. Passions are not always immediately clear and can evolve over time. Interests often change over time also. Take a moment now to write down what you feel is your purpose in life and what you are passionate about. Recording your thoughts and patterns that emerge during this self-reflection phase can be life-changing.

Explore and Experiment

Don't be afraid to try new things. Exploring different activities, volunteering, or even taking on new challenges can help you discover what truly excites and motivates you. Be open to new experiences, challenges, and opportunities that stretch your comfort zone and expand your horizons. Cultivate a mindset of curiosity, resilience, and adaptability that propels you toward personal and professional growth. Identify and write down your unique strengths, talents, and skills that set you apart and make you shine. Embrace your natural abilities and gifts. Consider how you can use them to make a positive impact in the world. By aligning your strengths with your purpose, you can create a life of authenticity and excellence.

Listen to Your Inner Voice

Pay attention to your intuitions and feelings. Sometimes, your inner voice can guide you toward your true passions and purpose. Meditation and mindfulness practices can help you connect more deeply with your inner self. Trust in your intuition to lead you toward the path that resonates with your soul. It might be uncomfortable, but that's when you will grow the most.

Seek Inspiration and Mentorship

Surround yourself with inspiration and mentorship from individuals who embody purpose and passion in their lives. Seek out role models, mentors, and guides who can offer wisdom, support, and encouragement. You can connect with them in person or online. Think of an area that you would like to explore and go to the bookstore to find books on the subject. Also, think of an area that you want to learn about, then reach out to others who are already doing it and introduce yourself. Be bold. This is your time.

Seek Feedback

Ask friends, family, or mentors for their insights into your strengths and what they think you are passionate about. Sometimes others can see our gifts and passions more clearly than we can. I did this recently with each of my children. It was very insightful for me. Seeking feedback from trusted individuals can be an invaluable step in the journey to finding your purpose. Here's why it's important:

Gaining Perspectives

Trusted friends, family members, or mentors can provide different perspectives on your strengths and talents. They might see skills or attributes in you that you haven't recognized yourself, offering you clarity and direction.

Confirming Authenticity

Sometimes, those who know you well can help you discern whether your pursuits truly align with your authentic self. They can spot when you seem genuinely engaged or when you're following a path that doesn't suit you.

Identifying Your Weaknesses

Feedback from others can help you identify areas where you might need growth or improvement. This awareness is crucial for personal development and aligning your actions with your true purpose.

Providing Encouragement

Trusted individuals can offer encouragement and support, validating your efforts and boosting your confidence as you explore different paths. They might also know someone to refer you to as you explore.

Challenging Assumptions

People who care about you can challenge assumptions you may hold about what you can or cannot do, helping you to push beyond self-imposed limitations.

Providing Accountability

Sharing your purpose exploration with a trusted group can create a sense of accountability. They can help motivate you to stay committed to exploring and pursuing your purpose.

Enhancing Self-Reflection

Engaging in dialogue and receiving constructive feedback can enhance self-reflection, prompting you to consider new angles and refine your understanding of your purpose. This is all about living authentically.

Encouraging Open Dialogue

Regular feedback fosters an ongoing dialogue about your journey, allowing continuous reassessment and adaptation of your goals as you grow and evolve to deepen your joy. Sometimes we might not like what we hear, but a trusted individual will help you grow.

The journey of finding your purpose is an empowering process that involves self-discovery; alignment with values, passions, and strengths; and a commitment to living a life of authenticity, joy, and impact. By engaging in self-reflection, identifying values and beliefs, following passions, embracing strengths, setting meaningful goals, listening to intuition, seeking inspiration, embracing growth, practicing gratitude and mindfulness, and taking aligned action, you can embark on a journey of self-discovery and fulfillment that leads you to your purpose. It empowers you to lead a life that is meaningful, fulfilling, and impactful. Embracing your purpose is a powerful way to achieve sustained joy and a sense of contentment, as it connects you to your true self and to the greater good of the world around you. Embrace the process with openness, curiosity, and courage. Finding your purpose and passion is a lifelong journey that significantly enhances your quality of life.

Living a Purpose-Driven Life

In a world where we often juggle multiple roles and face unique challenges, discovering and living a purpose-driven life can be a powerful catalyst for personal growth, fulfillment, and empowerment. Here are several reasons why it is crucial for us to live with purpose and passion:

Enhanced Well-Being

Living with a clear sense of purpose can significantly enhance mental, emotional, and physical well-being. When you align your daily activities with your core values and passions, you will experience greater satisfaction and joy. This alignment reduces stress and anxiety, as you are more likely to engage in activities that resonate with you and are less likely to feel pressured by external expectations. Additionally, purposeful living often encourages healthier lifestyle choices, such as regular exercise and balanced nutrition, further contributing to overall well-being.

Increased Resilience

Life is filled with challenges, and we often face obstacles related to gender roles, work-life balance, and societal expectations. A strong sense of purpose serves as an anchor during turbulent times, providing the strength and motivation needed to overcome adversity. When you have a clear understanding of your purpose, you are better equipped to navigate setbacks, view challenges as opportunities for growth, and maintain a positive outlook.

Empowerment and Confidence

Living a purpose-driven life empowers you by affirming your self-worth and capabilities. Pursuing goals and passions that are deeply meaningful to you fosters a sense of accomplishment and self-efficacy. This empowerment translates into increased confidence, enabling you to advocate for yourself, take on leadership roles, and make informed decisions about your life and future. Confident individuals are more likely to challenge societal norms, break free from limiting beliefs, and inspire change.

Meaningful Contributions to Society

People who live with purpose and passion often make significant contributions to their communities and society at large. Whether through professional achievements, volunteer work, or personal projects, purpose-driven individuals inspire positive change and create a ripple effect of impact. These contributions enrich society, promote social progress, and pave the way for future generations to thrive.

Role Modeling and Inspiration

Purpose-driven individuals serve as powerful role models for their peers, children, and the broader community. They demonstrate the value of pursuing one's passions, living authentically, and overcoming obstacles. This inspiration encourages others to seek their own purpose and strive for fulfillment, creating a culture of empowerment and personal growth. Younger generations benefit from seeing strong, purpose-driven individuals who lead by example.

Work-Life Balance

A clear sense of purpose helps you to prioritize what truly matters to you, facilitating better decision-making regarding career choices, relationships, and lifestyle. This clarity enables you to achieve a more harmonious balance between work, family, and personal interests. By focusing on activities that align with your values and passions, you can reduce burnout, increase productivity, and lead a more balanced life.

Fulfillment and Happiness

Ultimately, living a purpose-driven life leads to profound fulfillment and joy. When you engage in activities that resonate with your passions and values, you will experience a deep sense of contentment and purpose. This fulfillment permeates all aspects of life, enhancing relationships, work satisfaction, and overall happiness.

Living a purpose-driven life is transformative. It enhances well-being, fosters resilience, empowers, instills confidence, facilitates meaningful contributions to society, serves as inspiration for

others, promotes work-life balance, and leads to profound fulfillment and happiness. Embracing a purpose-driven life allows you
to navigate life's complexities with passion and direction, creating
a rich lasting joy and impactful existence that benefits both the
individual and the broader community.

ACTION ITEMS

Take fifteen minutes to write down what you think your purpose in life is. If you aren't sure, brainstorm and write down whatever you come up with.

_____

_____

_____

_____

What are your current passions and interests?

_____

_____

_____

What new interests would you like to explore?

_____

_____

_____

Who is in your trusted circle?

_____

_____

_____

_____

CHAPTER 7

GOAL SETTING TO
ACHIEVE MORE JOY

Take a Personal Inventory

L et's get started. Now that you understand the importance of exploring your purpose and passions, let's move on to the next step. One of the first steps to rekindling your joy is to step outside your box and look at yourself. Look in the mirror. Take a long, serious look at where you are and where you desire to be. Are you living the life you desire? What areas of your life need to be improved?

Get a piece of paper and draw a big circle and divide it into sections like a pie. Write down a different area of your life in each slice, such as family, friends, finances, relationships, career, spiritual, and so forth. Just sit back and look at each area. Write in the goals you have for each area. Then give a percentage to each area/slice that matches where you are currently in your goals for each area of your pie. Are you thinking about all the things that are meaningful and worthwhile to you? Are they based on purpose and passions? Periodically, bring out that wheel of life and see how much you are improving in each section. Most of us don't even know what's possible for us. We are too busy on our treadmill of life to think about all the possibilities out there.

Knowing your purpose and passions is of utmost importance and is the foundation of your life. Now you need to set concrete goals and strategies to get where you want to go. The goals you set are the milestones on your journey. They hold you accountable. I hate to be the bearer of bad news, but more joy doesn't just show up. To feel real joy, you need to be your best self, so you are fulfilled and are leaving the legacy you desire. Take the time to look through a new lens. Evaluate where you are and what areas you desire to make some changes in.

Goal Setting: The Power of the Bullseye

To grow, we must have short-term goals and long-term goals. A crystal-clear vision allows you to have clarity with your goals. It's time to develop your roadmap. Sit down and write out your priorities in life. Then write down six-month, one-year, two-year, and possibly five-year goals. Next, break it down into strategies to meet each goal: How are you going to meet the goal? What resources and time will be needed? Be kind to yourself. Everything takes time. Set realistic time frames to reach your goals.

Keep laser focused on each goal and strategy. What does this look like on your road map to life? The key is to take baby steps every day toward your goal, no matter how small or how big. Stay focused and consistent. There is no need to share it with others until you feel the time is right. You don't want to open yourself up to others who might try to dim your light by making negative comments, but it's always good to share your goals with those who support you. This goal setting practice will help to keep you accountable. When you are in control of your direction, you will soar and be a positive force for yourself and others.

An important part of goal setting is research. If you are planning a business, for example, you must first have some experience of what it will actually be like. Try to find someone who is in the role you want to be in to shadow for at least one day. Sit down with people who have had the experience you are aiming for. Read books about it, listen to podcasts, get a glimpse into the world you are headed for. It will help you anchor your thoughts more deeply and set the path to get where you want to go. I know that with the proper goal setting practices, you can attain any dream you truly want to achieve. It is never too late.

The Importance of Knowing Your Why

In the process of discovering more joy, it is important, of course, to know where you want to go on your journey of life, but it's also important to attach your *why*. I cannot emphasize this enough. Your why is the fuel in your life. For example, if you want to make more money, your why might be to provide a top-notch education to your children. Or it could be so you can be free of financial stress and travel the world. It's not just about money; it's about having a clear vision of attaining your goals and *why*.

Whatever you want to achieve in life, a why needs to be attached to that desire. If you are not fulfilled where you are today, setting goals are for the purpose of creating the life you desire. This new journey is so you can live a life with more fulfillment and joy. It is your why that will keep you anchored in your change. This will keep you more focused. What are you doing today and why?

Where do you want to go and why? When you are clear about your why, it serves as a guiding light that fuels your passion, determination, and resilience in pursuing your goals and finding your joy. Knowing your why provides a sense of direction, clarity, and meaning to your endeavors, helping you stay focused and committed, especially during challenging times. It aligns your actions with your values and beliefs, leading to a more fulfilling and purpose-driven life. Your why anchors your thoughts. Visualize it as a yellow Post-it on your forehead. Be committed to continuous improvement, focus on your why, and set your intentions.

I encourage you to make a vision board. For those who might not know what a vision board is, it's a corkboard, dry-erase board, chalkboard, or even a poster board. You write your goals and add pictures and quotes that motivate you and reinforce your why. Have your why all over it to keep you accountable and on track in the quest to rekindle your joy. For example, if you know you want to travel, take time to research, cut out pictures of where you want to go, and put them on your vision board. How does it make you feel when you look at the pictures? Anchor yourself in those thoughts and feelings.

Your why is your *north star*. It is your guiding principle or personal mission statement that represents your goals, visions, and purpose in life. It serves as a constant reference point that helps you stay on course, navigate challenges, and make decisions aligned with your core values and aspirations. Just as sailors use the North Star to find their way in the vast ocean, your personal north star guides you toward your true north, providing clarity and direction in both your personal and professional journeys. It acts as a beacon of light that illuminates your path, inspires you to strive for excellence, and reminds you of what truly matters to you. Developing a strong connection to your north star can empower you to live authentically, pursue your passions whole-heartedly, and create a life that is meaningful and fulfilling. Let your light shine brightly!

Be Your Own Driver: Taking Control of Your Life

As you navigate this path, it's essential to recognize that you are the driver of your life, the one in control of your choices, actions, and destiny. We need to quit blaming others for our unfulfilling lives. The life process comes from self. It is the self who can make it or break it. Your choices define you. So, what does it mean to be the driver of your life, and how can you take charge of your journey? Embracing responsibility means acknowledging that you can influence the direction of your life through the choices you make, the habits you cultivate, and the mindset you adopt. By taking ownership of your life, you reclaim your destiny, autonomy, and power to design a life that aligns with your values, passions, and purpose.

It's important to pay attention to your thoughts, emotions, and behaviors, and reflect on how they impact your well-being and relationships. Journal these thoughts. By practicing mindfulness, you can work on staying present in the moment, make conscious choices, and respond to challenges with clarity, composure, and resilience.

As the driver of your life, you must navigate challenges with courage, adaptability, and perseverance. Embrace setbacks as opportunities for growth, learn from failures, and approach obstacles with a solution-oriented mindset. How you get up after you fall is most important. By viewing challenges as stepping stones toward personal development and resilience, you can overcome adversity and emerge stronger on the other side.

Being the driver of your life means committing to continuous growth, learning, and self-improvement. Stay curious, openminded, and willing to explore new possibilities, ideas, and experiences. Invest in your personal and professional development, seek out mentors and role models, and challenge yourself to step outside your comfort zone. Decide what you won't do or accept. Learn to say no when it does not serve you in this new phase of your life. By embracing growth and learning, you expand your horizons, unlock your potential, and evolve into the best version of yourself.

Embracing change and adaptability in life is dynamic and ever-changing. I urge you to be flexible, resilient, and open to new opportunities, experiences, and perspectives. Embrace uncertainty as a natural part of growth, and welcome change as a chance to evolve, innovate, and transform. By embracing change with a positive attitude and a growth mindset, you can navigate life's transitions with grace and optimism. By recognizing your role as the architect of your reality, you empower yourself to design a life that reflects your values, aspirations, and dreams. Change comes with consistency. Remember, you hold the keys to your destiny. You are the author of your life and your story.

Energy Vampires

We are all surrounded by energy vampires—watch out for them! They can be a coworker, a friend, a family member, or even a partner. I am sure you have had conversations that exhaust you. That's an interaction with an energy vampire. I know that I have been an energy vampire to close family and friends at times. There is a wonderful book by Jon Gordon called *The Energy Bus*. It is a thought-provoking book. I urge you to read it. In addition to lots of other great, enlightening information, he discusses energy vampires in our lives. You will always have negativity show up in your life, but you need to learn to respond with high positivity. It will throw them. I was trained by a mentor to notice when the hair on my neck begins to flare, walk away. Don't get involved. Once someone starts talking without taking a breath, you know they might be an energy vampire. Know yourself and how to walk away gracefully without getting involved. It's for your own sanity. Protect your space and establish your guardrails. You need your full energy for your quest to find more joy.

Seize Opportunities

Once you clear your mind, set your intentions, and open your heart, you will see that we are all surrounded by abundance and blessings. So, make a strong effort to open your heart and mind to expect opportunities. You will be able to experience these wonderful blessings more clearly. They will happen. Don't let opportunities pass you by. New opportunities might be a little scary, but that's only because you are out of your comfort zone. It's OK. Get comfortable with being uncomfortable. Remember growth will not happen until you are uncomfortable. The problem is that most of us don't want to feel uncomfortable. We don't want to take risks, and prefer to sit in our own comfort zone. That is why many of us are stagnated and not growing. So, you can do this! Believe in yourself and follow your chosen roadmap.

Take some time in a quiet space to examine your core beliefs. Write your thoughts daily, no matter how short or long. Ask yourself this thought-provoking question: What has your hesitation cost you in life? I am not talking just about financial costs, but the opportunities and potential growth you might have missed out on due to your indecision or fear of taking the next step. Time is a precious resource. Hesitation can lead to significant delays, which could have been used to make progress, develop skills, and achieve goals. Reflecting on what has potentially been lost or delayed due to hesitation can be a powerful motivator to take more decisive actions in the future. It's a way to remind yourself that growth often comes from making bold moves and embracing challenges.

Remember, as you feel you are becoming a better version of you, joy will set in. You will feel lighter in your chest and in your mind. Your world will begin to radiate light. I ask you to make a daily routine of writing in your journal. It's a new launchpad for you. Remember that your past does not predict your future—don't look back. I heard one time that history is not a place of residence but a place of reference. This is such a great way to look at and think about your life.

ACTION ITEMS

What is holding you back from living your full potential?

_____

_____

_____

_____

Clearly write five goals you would like to attain. Remember to attach your why. Then write the strategies to achieve each goal.

_____

_____

_____

_____

Who are you going to share your goals with to keep you accountable?

_____

_____

_____

_____

What are you passionate about?

_____

_____

_____

_____

Who are the energy vampires in your life?

_____

_____

_____

_____

Make your vision board and post pictures of your passions and your goals.

_____

_____

_____

_____

CHAPTER 8

BUILDING RESILIENCE

The Connection Between Resilience and Joy

Resilience is the capacity for you to recover quickly from difficulties and adapt in the face of adversity, trauma, or significant sources of stress. It embodies your mental, emotional, and behavioral flexibility to manage setbacks, challenges, and change in a positive and effective manner. Resilience is not an inherent trait that you either have or don't have; rather, it involves behaviors, thoughts, and actions that can be learned and developed by anyone. Resilience is closely interconnected with joy in several meaningful ways. It helps you bounce back from adversity and maintain a positive outlook in tough situations. Resilience helps you manage stress and negative emotions; it helps you see challenges as opportunities for growth and learning, which can lead to a deeper sense of satisfaction and joy. This multifaceted effect of resilience often helps you build strong, supportive relationships, which are a key source of joy and fulfillment; it also helps you believe in your own ability to handle whatever comes your way, leading to a sense of empowerment and joy.

Gratitude Practice

Gratitude and resilience have a mutually reinforcing relationship. Research suggests that practicing gratitude can enhance an individual's resilience by promoting a positive mindset, reducing stress, and improving emotional well-being. When you focus on what you are grateful for, you are often more equipped to handle adversities, as gratitude fosters optimism and empowers you to see challenges as opportunities for growth. Conversely, resilience can also enhance your capacity for gratitude. Those who build resilience tend to navigate challenges more effectively, resulting in an increased appreciation for the positive aspects of life, even amid difficulties. Thus, seeing your ability to bounce back can lead to greater awareness and expression of gratitude.

Purposeful Living

Resilience can lead you to a more purpose-driven life, where pursuing meaningful goals and interests brings you lasting joy. It gives you a greater sense of meaning and direction. When you have a clear purpose, you possess a guiding north star. This sense of direction helps you navigate challenges and maintain focus during difficult times, contributing to greater resilience.

Purposeful living encourages you to set meaningful goals aligned with your values and passions. This focus not only motivates you to persevere but also builds resilience by fostering a proactive approach to overcoming obstacles. Research also suggests that individuals with a strong sense of purpose experience higher levels of emotional well-being. Positive emotions, in turn, bolster resilience by providing the emotional resources needed to cope with stress and adversity.

Reduced Fear of Failure

Resilience reduces fear of failure, which can make you more willing to take risks and pursue things that bring you joy. Here are some ideas for you to reduce your fear of failure so you can build better resilience:

Reframe Fear as Opportunity

View fear as a signal that you are stepping out of your comfort zone, which is where growth happens. By shifting your perspective on fear, you can transform it into a catalyst for positive change.

Gradual Exposure

Face your fears in small, manageable steps. By gradually exposing yourself to what you fear, you can become more comfortable and build confidence over time.

Mindfulness and Relaxation

Practice mindfulness activities such as meditation or deep breathing to manage anxiety. Staying present can help you avoid getting overwhelmed by fear.

So, how do you know if you are resilient? Here are some key traits and behaviors that may indicate you are resilient:

- Positive attitude: You maintain a positive outlook even in challenging situations.

- Adaptability: You can adjust to new circumstances and pivot when necessary.

- Problem-solving skills: You approach problems methodically, finding effective solutions.

- Self-awareness: You understand your strengths and weaknesses and use them to your advantage.

- Good emotional regulation: You manage your emotions effectively, staying calm under pressure.

- Perseverance: You persist in the face of obstacles without giving up easily.

- Strong support network: You have a group of friends, family members, or colleagues you can rely on.

- Regular self-care: You prioritize your physical, emotional, and mental well-being.

- Growth mindset: You believe in continuous learning and personal development.

- Purpose: You have a clear sense of purpose and direction in your life.

Here are some practical tips for you in building mental strength to enhance resilience:

Practice Self-Awareness

Developing self-awareness involves understanding your thoughts, emotions, and behaviors. Regularly reflecting on your experiences can help you identify patterns that contribute to stress or undermine your resilience. Journaling is an excellent tool for cultivating self-awareness. Write down your thoughts and feelings each day and review them to gain insights into your emotional responses and coping strategies.

Cultivate a Growth Mindset

A *growth mindset*, a term coined by psychologist Carol Dweck, is the belief that abilities and intelligence can be developed through effort and learning. Embrace challenges as opportunities to grow rather than viewing them as insurmountable obstacles. When you encounter setbacks, ask yourself, "What can I learn from this experience?" Shifting your perspective in this way can foster resilience by making you more adaptable and open to change.

Develop Emotional Regulation Skills

Managing your emotions effectively is crucial for resilience. Techniques such as mindfulness, deep breathing exercises, and meditation can help you stay calm and focused under pressure. Practice these techniques regularly to build your emotional regulation skills. When faced with a stressful situation, take a few deep breaths or engage in a brief mindfulness exercise to center yourself.

Set Realistic Goals

Break down large tasks or goals into smaller, manageable steps daily. This approach allows you to make steady progress toward your goals and prevents feeling overwhelmed. Celebrate small victories along the way to maintain motivation and build confidence. This will build resilience as you see progress. Setting SMART (specific, measurable, achievable, relevant, and time-bound) goals can help you stay focused and achieve your objectives more effectively.

Strengthen Social Connections

Cultivate relationships with friends, family members, and colleagues who provide emotional support, encouragement, and practical help. Reach out to others during times of need and offer your support in return. Building and maintaining these connections can provide a sense of belonging and enhance your resilience.

Develop Problem-Solving Skills

Enhance your ability to face challenges head-on by improving your problem-solving skills. When confronting a difficult situation, take a systematic approach: Define the problem, brainstorm potential solutions, evaluate the pros and cons of each option, and choose an action plan. Practice this method regularly to build your confidence in handling adversity.

Practice Gratitude

Cultivating gratitude can enhance resilience by shifting your focus from what's going wrong to what's going right. Regularly acknowledging the positive aspects of your life can boost your mood and overall outlook. Keep writing about your gratitude in your journal daily and make a habit of writing down three things you are grateful for each day. This practice can help you maintain a positive perspective, even during challenging times.

Seek Professional Help When Needed

If you find yourself struggling to cope with stress or adversity, consider seeking help from a mental health professional. Therapists and counselors can provide valuable support and guidance, helping you develop effective coping strategies and build resilience.

Developing mental strength is crucial for building resilience and navigating life's challenges with grace. By practicing self-awareness, cultivating a growth mindset, developing healthy habits, regulating emotions, setting realistic goals, strengthening social connections, enhancing problem-solving skills, practicing gratitude, and seeking professional help when needed, you can enhance your mental resilience and thrive in the face of adversity. Resilience is a crucial attribute that impacts all aspects of life, from mental and physical health to relationships and personal achievements. Cultivating resilience through developing mental strength is a key component of resilience, enabling you to withstand adversity, recover, and thrive on the road to finding your joy.

Linking Resilience to Physical Health and Regular Exercise

Resilience is often thought of in mental and emotional terms, but physical health and regular exercise play a crucial role in building and maintaining your resilience. The connection between physical health and resilience is profound, as a healthy body can better withstand stress, recover from illness, and adapt to change. Here are several ways that physical health and regular exercise contribute to your enhanced resilience:

Stress Reduction

Regular exercise is one of the most effective ways to combat stress. By maintaining a regular exercise routine, no matter how small or big, you can keep your stress levels in check, making it easier to cope with life's challenges. Taking a short daily walk can improve your energy and outlook on life. If you aren't able to walk, you can do exercises in a chair. The idea is to just get moving. A Mayo Clinic article titled "Exercise and Stress: Get Moving to Manage Stress" states that exercise in almost any form can act as a stress reliever.[xii] Another article, written by Emma Childs and Harriet de Wit and published in the journal *Frontiers of Physiology* in 2014, says that regular exercise is associated with emotional resilience to acute stress in healthy adults.[xiii]

Improved Mood and Emotional Health

Exercise has been shown to alleviate symptoms of depression and anxiety. Engaging in regular physical activity can help boost your self-esteem and improve overall mood through the release of neurotransmitters like serotonin and dopamine. Enhanced emotional health fosters resilience by creating a stable foundation from which to tackle adversity.

Better Sleep

Adequate sleep is essential for physical and mental recovery. Regular exercise helps regulate sleep patterns, ensuring that you get the restorative sleep you need. Quality sleep enhances cognitive function, mood, and energy levels, all of which are critical for resilient behavior and effective problem-solving. Good sleep hygiene helps improve your sleep. That is a set of practices and habits that are conducive to achieving consistent, restorative, and high-quality sleep. Here are some key elements of good sleep hygiene:

Consistent Sleep Schedule

Go to bed and wake up at the same time every day, including weekends, to help regulate your body's internal clock.

Relaxing Bedtime Routine

Engage in calming activities before bed, such as reading or taking a warm bath, to signal to your body that it's time to wind down.

Comfortable Sleep Environment

Ensure your bedroom is conducive to sleep, with a comfortable mattress and pillows, a cool room temperature, and minimal noise and light.

Limiting Screen Time

Reduce exposure to screens such as phones, tablets, and computers at least an hour before bed, as the blue light emitted can interfere with melatonin production and sleep cycles.

Mindful Eating and Drinking

Avoid large meals, caffeine, and alcohol close to bedtime, as these can disrupt sleep.

Physical Activity

Engaging in regular physical activity during the day can promote better sleep, but it's often recommended to avoid vigorous exercise close to bedtime.

Managing Stress

Incorporate stress-reduction techniques such as mindfulness, meditation, or deep breathing exercises to alleviate anxiety that might interfere with sleep.

Exercise not only helps with sleep but has a host of other benefits as well. Here are some:

Enhanced Cognitive Function

Physical activity has been linked to improved brain function and cognitive abilities. Exercise increases blood flow to the brain, promoting the growth of new neurons and enhancing neuroplasticity. This results in better memory, concentration, and problem-solving skills, making it easier to navigate complex situations and adapt to change.

Strengthened Immune System

Regular exercise strengthens our immune system by improving circulation and promoting the efficient functioning of organs. A strong immune system reduces the likelihood of illness and speeds up recovery, enabling you to bounce back more quickly from physical setbacks and maintain overall resilience.

Physical Strength and Stamina

Building physical strength and stamina through regular exercise translates to greater endurance and energy levels. This physical robustness enables you to handle the demands of daily life more easily and recover from physical challenges more rapidly, enhancing overall resilience.

Healthy Habits and Discipline

Maintaining a regular exercise regime cultivates discipline and healthy habits. This self-regulation translates into other areas of our lives, promoting better time management, goal setting, and adherence to healthy routines. These skills are essential for developing resilience.

Social Connection

Participating in group sports or exercise classes helps build social connections and support networks. These connections provide us emotional support and a sense of community, which are vital components of resilience. Social interactions also provide opportunities for encouragement and motivation, reinforcing the commitment to regular exercise.

Bottom line: The relationship between physical health, regular exercise, and resilience is multifaceted. By engaging in consistent physical activity, you can reduce stress, improve emotional health, enhance cognitive function, and build physical strength. These benefits collectively contribute to a more resilient disposition, enabling you to better manage life's challenges and recover from setbacks. Incorporating exercise into daily routines is a powerful strategy for fostering resilience and promoting a healthier, more balanced life.

ACTION ITEMS

Write down three achievable actions that can strengthen your resilience.

_____

_____

_____

_____

Write down three to five times when you were faced with obstacles and how you persevered.

_____

_____

_____

_____

Do you see yourself adapting well to change? If not, write down some actions you can take to become more flexible and adaptable.

_____

_____

_____

_____

Schedule in exercise on your calendar three to four times a week and write down what type of exercise you will start today! Remember, even a short walk is great to start with to build resilience.

_____

_____

_____

_____

CHAPTER 9

THE CONNECTION OF JOY TO MINDFULNESS AND MEDITATION

Let's delve into mindfulness more deeply. Mindfulness has become an increasingly popular practice in modern society, but its roots extend back thousands of years, drawing from ancient traditions such as Buddhism and yoga. At its core mindfulness involves the practice of paying intentional, non-judgmental attention to the present moment. It is about being aware of where you are and what you are doing, and noticing if you are being reactive or overwhelmed by what's going on around you.

Mindfulness can be defined as a state of active, open attention to the present. This means you observe thoughts and feelings without judging them as good or bad—just noticing them. Instead of letting life pass by unnoticed, mindfulness empowers you to live in the moment and be fully engaged with your surroundings.

One time I was hosting a world-renowned physician for the day. I picked him up from the airport, and we went to have breakfast nearby. After we were done, he said, "Let's take a walk." I had no idea why. Well, we walked through a park and a shopping

THE POWER OF JOY

center just looking and observing. I thought, *What the heck is going on?* When we finally got back in the car forty-five minutes later, he said, "Wasn't that delightful?" He was practicing mindfulness to get grounded before attending all the business meetings that were planned. That was an aha day for me.

Practicing mindfulness regularly can bring about numerous benefits for your mental, emotional, and physical well-being. Meditation and mindfulness are powerful practices that can significantly enhance feelings of joy and overall well-being. Here's how they are interconnected:

Reduce Stress

The practices of meditation and mindfulness can both lower stress levels. One of the most well-researched benefits of mindfulness is its ability to reduce stress. There was a study done at UC Davis that showed mindfulness from meditation is associated with lower levels of a stress hormone. Mindfulness practices can lower our levels of cortisol, the body's main stress hormone, promoting a calmer, more relaxed state. By focusing on the present moment, you can lessen your preoccupation with past regrets and future anxieties.

Increased Awareness

Mindfulness helps you become more aware of the present moment, allowing you to savor joyful experiences more fully. Mindfulness encourages self-exploration and reflection, helping you gain deeper insights into your thoughts, feelings, and behaviors. This self-awareness is crucial for personal growth and development, as it allows you to recognize patterns and make conscious changes.

Emotional Regulation

Meditation helps in managing emotions effectively, reducing feelings of anxiety and depression, and making room for more joy. Mindfulness helps you become more aware of your emotional responses and develop healthier ways to manage them. By observing your emotions without judgment, you can reduce impulsivity and react to situations more thoughtfully. This leads to improved relationships and a more balanced emotional life.

Enhanced Gratitude

Mindfulness fosters a greater appreciation for the small pleasures in life, boosting overall happiness and joy.

Improved Focus

Both practices enhance your ability to focus, which can lead to better productivity and a sense of accomplishment, contributing to joy. Regular mindfulness practice can improve attention and concentration. By training your mind to focus on a single task or sensation at a time, you can become better at sustaining your attention and ignoring distractions. This is especially beneficial in today's fast-paced world, where multitasking is common.

Positive Thinking

Meditation encourages positive thinking patterns, which can increase your overall sense of joy. Regular meditation cultivates a sense of inner peace and contentment, which is a foundation for lasting joy.

Better Relationships

Mindfulness improves empathy and communication, which can lead to more fulfilling and joyful relationships. Mindfulness promotes being present with others so you can listen more deeply and respond more genuinely, enhancing your connection and communication.

Resilience

These practices can build resilience, helping you to bounce back from difficulties and maintain a joyful outlook. Greater mindfulness builds your resilience by fostering a nonreactive, accepting attitude toward life's challenges. By learning to observe difficulties without becoming overwhelmed, you can navigate stress and adversity more effectively.

Improved Mental Health

Mindfulness has been shown to have significant positive effects on various mental health conditions, including depression and anxiety. It helps you develop greater emotional awareness and regulation, which can lead to decreased symptoms of these disorders. Techniques such as mindfulness-based stress reduction (MBSR) and mindfulness-based cognitive therapy (MBCT) have been particularly effective in treating depression and preventing relapse.[xiv] There are many studies by David Creswell on mindfulness and improved mental health.

Enhanced Physical Health

The benefits of mindfulness extend to physical health as well. It can help lower blood pressure, improve sleep quality, reduce chronic pain, and boost the immune system. The practice of mindful eating can also lead you to healthier eating habits and better digestion by promoting awareness of hunger and satisfaction cues.

Bottom line: Mindfulness and meditation are powerful practices that can significantly enhance your quality of life. By cultivating present-moment awareness, you can experience reduced stress, improved mental and physical health, better emotional regulation, and stronger relationships. Embracing mindfulness is a step toward a more balanced, fulfilling life which in turn will bring you everlasting joy. There are many resources on mindful. org to help you in your practice of mindfulness.

Simple Meditation and Mindfulness Exercises

Meditation and mindfulness are accessible practices that anyone can incorporate into their daily routine to develop inner peace, enhance focus, and improve emotional well-being. Here are some simple exercises that you can start with. I encourage you to weave them into your daily routines.

Basic Mindfulness Meditation

Find a quiet space: Choose a comfortable place where you won't be disturbed.

Sit comfortably: Sit in a chair or on the floor on a cushion so your hips are higher than your knees, with your back straight but not rigid. Place your hands on your knees or in your lap.

Set a timer: Start with five minutes. As you become more comfortable, you can gradually extend the time.

Focus on your breath: Close your eyes or keep your eyes open, whichever brings you the most comfort and focus. Notice the sensation of the air entering and leaving your nostrils, the rise and fall of your chest or abdomen. When your mind wanders, notice, label it *thinking* in your mind, and gently bring your focus back to your breath without judgment.

This practice helps cultivate patience and concentration. There are many different breathing practices. Explore and find the breathing exercise that is best for you and integrate the practice of mindfulness into your day-to-day activities. Find the practice that makes you most comfortable.

Body Scan Meditation

Lie down comfortably: Lie on your back with your legs uncrossed and arms at your sides, palms facing up.

Focus on breathing: Take a few deep breaths, inhaling and exhaling, then let your breath settle into its natural rhythm.

Scan your body: Starting at the top of your head, slowly moving your focus through each part of your body, notice any sensations of tension, discomfort, or relaxation. Move through your forehead, eyes, jaw, neck, shoulders, arms, chest, abdomen, legs, and feet.

Acknowledge sensations: Simply observe without trying to change anything.

This practice helps deepen your awareness of physical sensations and promotes relaxation.

Mindful Breathing

Sit comfortably: Find a comfortable sitting position, either on a chair or cross-legged on a cushion on the floor.

Take deep breaths: Inhale deeply through your nose, allowing your belly to expand. Exhale slowly through your mouth. Count your breaths silently. Count slowly up to five for the inhale, and down from five for the exhale. You can increase the count as you become comfortable. When your mind wanders, gently guide it back to your breath and keep counting.

This exercise helps center your mind and reduce anxiety.

Walking Meditation

Find a quiet path: Choose a tranquil place where you can walk without interruptions. You can even walk in circles around your kitchen table. Begin walking at a slow and steady pace.

Focus on each step: Notice sensations. Pay attention to the sensations in your feet as they contact the ground, lift off, and move forward. As you become more comfortable, expand your awareness to include your surroundings—the sensation of the breeze, the sounds of nature, the smell of the air. When your mind drifts, gently bring it back to the act of walking.

This practice helps you stay present and connected to the moment.

Loving-Kindness Meditation (Metta)

Sit comfortably: Find a comfortable sitting position and close your eyes. Focus on your breath. Take a few deep breaths, inhaling and exhaling to settle into the practice.

Recite phrases of kindness: Silently repeat phrases such as "I am happy. I am healthy. I live with ease and joy." Direct these phrases first toward yourself. Gradually extend these wishes to others, first to someone you love, then to a neutral person, and finally to someone with whom you have difficulty.

Feel the kindness: Focus on the feelings of compassion and kindness as you repeat the phrases.

This exercise fosters emotional resilience and empathy.

Mindful Eating

Choose a food item: Select a piece of fruit, a small snack, or even a meal. Observe it mindfully. Before eating, take a moment to observe the color, texture, and smell of the food.

Chew slowly: Take small bites and chew slowly, noticing the flavors and textures. Be present.

Focus entirely on the act of eating: Avoid distractions like TV or smartphones.

This practice enhances appreciation and mindful engagement with the present moment.

Incorporating meditation and mindfulness exercises into your daily routine can significantly enhance your mental and emotional well-being. These simple practices are powerful tools for cultivating a calm, centered, and resilient mind.

Mindful Movements

Mindful movement refers to physical activities that integrate movement with mindfulness principles, promoting both physical health and mental well-being. This practice encourages being fully present during movement, creating an awareness of the body's sensations, alignment, and breath. For all of us, mindful movement can be particularly beneficial, offering a holistic approach to managing stress, enhancing fitness, and nurturing self-compassion and body positivity. Here are some key mindful movement practices and their benefits:

Yoga

Yoga is perhaps the most well-known form of mindful movement. It combines physical postures, breath control, and meditation. You can go to a yoga studio or do it in the privacy of your own home. There are many studies about the effects of yoga, mindfulness, and meditation on telomere activity. Telomeres play a critical role in maintaining the stability of our DNA during cell division. As cells divide over our lifetime, telomeres gradually shorten, which is associated with aging and, in some cases, diseases. Telomere length is an indicator of age-related health and well-being. Those of you who are interested in the area of longevity and well-being might want to read some of the research and articles in *Yoga Research and Beyond*. It's a great educational resource for you. Let's look at some of the other benefits of yoga.

Benefits include:

Flexibility and Strength

Yoga enhances flexibility and builds muscle strength through various postures (asanas).

Stress Relief

The focus on breath and movement coordination helps reduce stress, calm the mind, and improve overall mental health.

Body Awareness

Regular practice fosters a deep awareness of the body's alignment and movement patterns, promoting better posture and reducing the risk of injury. Individuals of all ages can benefit from yoga, whether it's a gentle hatha class or a more vigorous vinyasa flow.

Tai Chi and Qigong

Tai chi and qigong are traditional Chinese practices that involve slow, deliberate movements, breath control, and meditation.

Benefits include:

Balance and Coordination

These practices improve balance, coordination, and proprioception, which are essential for maintaining physical stability and preventing falls.

Mind-Body Connection

The slow, rhythmic movements enhance the mind-body connection, promoting relaxation and reducing anxiety. Both practices are believed to enhance the flow of qi (life energy) throughout the body, contributing to overall vitality and well-being. These gentle movements are suitable for individuals of all fitness levels and can be particularly beneficial for us as we age and for those recovering from injuries.

Dance Meditation

Dance meditation combines free-form dancing with mindfulness and meditation techniques.

Benefits include:

Emotional Expression

Dance allows for creative expression and emotional release, which can be incredibly therapeutic.

Joy and Connection

Dancing can evoke feelings of joy, freedom, and connection to oneself and others.

As a form of joyful movement, dance encourages you to appreciate your body for its abilities rather than its appearance. Whether it's a structured class or just dancing freely at home, dance can be a liberating and empowering practice.

Pilates

Pilates focuses on core strength, flexibility, and mindful movement.
Benefits include:

Core Stability

Pilates strengthens the core muscles, essential for overall stability and preventing injuries.

Mindful Control

Emphasis on precision and control encourages mindful awareness of each movement.

Postural Alignment

The practice helps improve posture, alleviate back pain, and promote a balanced body.

Pilates can be particularly beneficial for you if you are looking to build strength, enhance flexibility, and improve overall body alignment.

Overall, mindful movements offer you a holistic approach to well-being, addressing physical fitness, mental health, and emotional resilience. Practices like yoga, tai chi, dance meditation, Pilates, and walking meditation allow you to connect with your body, reduce stress, and cultivate a positive self-image. By integrating mindfulness into physical activity, you can create a balanced, fulfilling practice that supports your overall health and well-being. These all lead to finding more joy in your life.

ACTION ITEMS

What are the daily mindfulness practices you engage in now?

_____

_____

_____

_____

List three to five ways you will practice mindfulness going forward.

_____

_____

_____

_____

Schedule five to ten minutes on your calendar for meditation daily.

_____

_____

_____

_____

What mindful movement feels best for you? Commit to doing it for at least ten minutes a day.

_____

_____

_____

_____

Post mindful activities that will bring you more joy on your vision board. These will help you to remain focused.

_____

_____

_____

_____

CHAPTER 10

～ᴏ～

SELF-CARE AND JOY

Self-Care Is Not Optional

Even if you have all your goals and strategies set perfectly in place, there are some very foundational needs that you must fulfill as you design and follow your road map. Self-care is critical to catapulting yourself. When one begins to neglect their nutrition, exercise, and proper rest, depression starts to set in. Joy will dwindle because you are unhappy with the way you are thinking, feeling, and looking. Your light will surely disappear. There are several reasons why you might neglect self-care. Do any of these resonate with you?

Time Constraints

You feel you don't have enough time for self-care due to your busy schedule.

Guilt and Prioritization

You prioritize others' needs over your own, feeling guilty when you take time for yourself.

Lack of Awareness

You might not fully understand what self-care is or how it benefits you.

Cultural or Societal Pressures

There can be a perception that self-care is selfish or indulgent.

Mental Health Barriers

Depression or anxiety can make it difficult for you to prioritize or engage in self-care activities.

There is a lot of research showing how self-care can improve mental and physical health, increase productivity, and enhance relationships. Self-care is essential maintenance rather than a luxury, akin to charging a phone or servicing a car. It's important that you take time to reflect on areas of neglect in your life and how self-care could fill those gaps. Embarking on a self-care journey can feel overwhelming, but it begins with small, intentional steps that fit seamlessly into your daily routine. Here's a guide to help you get started:

Prioritize Time for Yourself

Begin by setting aside a specific time each day dedicated to self-care. It doesn't need to be long; even ten to fifteen minutes can make a difference. The key is consistency.

Identify Your Needs

Reflect on aspects of your life that could use nurturing. This might be physical (e.g., exercise, rest), emotional (e.g., journaling, meditating), or social (e.g., connecting with loved ones).

Start Small and Simple

Incorporate simple self-care activities like deep breathing, taking a walk, or drinking a glass of water mindfully. Small actions are easier to maintain and can evolve over time.

Create a Self-Care Plan

Write down activities you enjoy and integrate them into your routine. Having a plan and putting time on your calendar ensures you remain committed.

Set Boundaries

Learn to say no and protect your self-care time from unnecessary commitments. Boundaries allow you to recharge and prevent burnout.

Seek Support

Engage with a community, friend, or partner who supports your self-care journey. Sharing experiences can provide motivation and new ideas.

Evaluate and Adjust

Regularly assess how your self-care practices make you feel. If something isn't working, don't hesitate to try a new approach. Flexibility is key to a sustainable routine.

I urge you to take immediate charge of your self-care. Take time for yourself physically, emotionally, and mentally. Do activities that energize and renew you. They are essential to giving you clarity. Discovering self-care is one of the first important steps to rekindling your joy.

I went a long time in life not taking the time to practice self-care. I felt I didn't have the time or money for it. I had much more important things to do, like taking care of the children and working. I was wrong in my thinking. Now my children think of me as the queen of self-care! It is an amazing journey that can lead you to profound joy, inner peace, and a deep sense of fulfillment. When you develop a loving and compassionate relationship with yourself, you create a foundation for experiencing happiness and contentment in all areas of your life. I know this is a difficult concept for many of us, but it's a crucial part of living to your full potential.

Self-care truthfully is an act of self-love and self-compassion that honors your worth, value, and inherent dignity. By treating yourself with kindness, respect, and care, you deepen your connection to yourself, foster a sense of self-acceptance, and cultivate a positive relationship with your inner self. Self-care is an important life-changing practice that nurtures your well-being, enhances your life, and empowers you to live with vitality, balance, and joy. By prioritizing your needs, you create a foundation of resilience, vitality, and fulfillment that supports your overall health and happiness. Embrace the importance of self-care as a daily practice. Make self-care a nonnegotiable part of your routine. It's not a reward. Figure out what works best for you. Is it group exercise, daily walks, meditation, reading, journaling, or spending time in nature? It can be taking a bath or sitting down and having a warm cup of tea. Prioritizing self-care shows you that you are worthy of love and attention.

Engage in activities that bring you joy, fulfillment, and a sense of purpose. Pursue your passions, hobbies, and interests with enthusiasm and dedication. When you invest in activities that light you up, you cultivate a sense of joy and vitality that radiates from you, cultivating positive relationships. Surround yourself with positivity by cultivating relationships and environments that uplift and inspire you. Seek out supportive friends, mentors, and communities that encourage your growth and well-being. Surround yourself with positivity that nurtures self-love and joy. Develop relationships that are based on mutual respect, trust, and authenticity. Seek out friends, mentors, and loved ones who celebrate your uniqueness and encourage your growth.

Open communication with a partner is a crucial component of self-care, as it fosters mutual understanding, support, and trust. Practice open, honest communication in your relationships. Many of us do what we call emotional stacking. We keep holding our thoughts inside until one day we explode. It's very unhealthy for you and for your relationships. By communicating authentically, you create space for genuine connection, understanding, and intimacy with others. Truth gives you emotional freedom. It is your superpower. Clear your soul and open your heart. Let go of past hurts, grudges, and self-criticism. Practice forgiveness toward yourself and others to release emotional baggage and cultivate a sense of peace and acceptance. Forgiveness is a powerful act of self-love that frees you from the weight of resentment and allows you to move forward with an open heart. By changing your dialogue, you create space for self-love to thrive. Here are some tips that can guide you to enhance communication as part of your self-care:

Set the Intent

Set clear intentions for your communication, focusing on understanding and connection rather than winning an argument or being right.

Choose the Right Time

Always try to find an appropriate time to talk, when both you and your partner are relaxed and undistracted. Create an environment where meaningful conversation can take place.

Practice Active Listening

Even though it might be difficult, practice active listening, which involves paying full attention to your partner or friend, showing empathy, and reflecting back what you have heard to ensure understanding.

Be Honest but Kind

It's important to be honest about your feelings while being mindful of your partner's or friend's emotions. I suggest using a tone that is compassionate and supportive.

Maintain Open-Mindedness

Work hard to stay open-minded and show willingness to compromise. This helps build a partnership based on cooperation and mutual respect.

Express Appreciation

I cannot emphasize enough the importance of regularly expressing gratitude and appreciation to strengthen the bond and promote a positive communication climate.

Do Regular Check-Ins

Discuss how each person is feeling about their self-care goals and progress, reinforcing support and accountability.

Seek Outside Help if Needed

Last, seek the guidance of a therapist or counselor when facing communication challenges. Professional help can provide invaluable tools and insights.

Falling in love with yourself can be life-changing in your journey of self-discovery and self-acceptance. Self-care lays the foundation for healthy, fulfilling relationships with others. When you cultivate a deep sense of self-love and compassion, you are better equipped to give and receive love authentically, nurture meaningful connections, and create a life that is rich in joy, fulfillment, and harmony.

Take time to explore your values, beliefs, and aspirations. Identify what matters most to you, what brings you joy, and what aligns with your authentic self. Embrace your uniqueness and honor your values as guiding principles in your life. Be kind and gentle with yourself, especially in moments of self-doubt or vulnerability. Treat yourself with the same compassion and understanding you would offer to a dear friend. Embrace your imperfections and celebrate your strengths. Practice self-compassion by treating yourself with kindness, understanding, and empathy, especially during times of struggle or self-doubt. Be gentle with yourself, acknowledge your feelings without judgment, and offer yourself the same level of love and compassion you would give to a loved one.

Finding self-love and joy without feeling guilty is a life-changing process that involves releasing self-imposed limitations, embracing self-compassion, and prioritizing your well-being. By consistently nurturing yourself with these practices, you can build a strong foundation of self-love and live a more balanced, fulfilling life filled with joy.

ACTION ITEMS

In what ways do you practice self-care now?

_____

_____

_____

_____

Write down what you are going to do for self-care on a weekly and monthly basis. Schedule them on your calendar.

_____

_____

_____

_____

Write down three to five communication goals with your partner.

_____

_____

_____

_____

CHAPTER 11

EMPOWERING RELATIONSHIPS
LEAD TO GREATER JOY

Supportive and positive relationships are fundamental to our well-being and personal growth. They provide emotional support, reduce stress, and enhance our quality of life. Nurturing such relationships requires empathy, effort, and effective communication. Prioritize spending quality time together, whether it's through regular catch-ups, shared activities, or simply being present. Small acts of kindness, like offering help, giving compliments, or doing something special, can strengthen the bond and demonstrate care and affection. These will bring you joy. Here are some tips to help you cultivate and maintain strong, healthy relationships:

Prioritize Effective Communication

Practice active listening by giving your full attention to the person speaking, avoiding interruptions, and reflecting back what you've heard. This demonstrates respect and understanding. Focus on truly hearing and understanding the other person's perspective. Active listening involves giving full attention, nodding, and providing feedback that shows comprehension. It helps in building empathy and reducing misunderstandings.

Using *I* statements can help you communicate your needs without blaming or criticizing others. For example, "I feel upset when . . ." rather than "You always . . ." Pay attention to body language, eye contact, and tone of voice. These nonverbal cues often convey more than words and can enhance understanding and connection.

Show Empathy and Understanding

Try to understand things from the other person's perspective. Empathy involves recognizing and validating their emotions and experiences. Offer your support and understanding when someone is going through a challenging period. Sometimes, just being there to listen can make a significant difference. Keep your promises and follow through on commitments. Reliability builds trust and shows that you value the relationship.

Honesty is crucial for building trust. Be truthful, even when it's difficult, and encourage others to be honest with you. Recognize that everyone is unique and has different perspectives, values, and beliefs. Embrace these differences and avoid judging others. Empowering relationships take time to develop and grow. Practice patience and give each other the time and space needed to strengthen your bond.

Offer Genuine Appreciation and Gratitude

Regularly acknowledge and express gratitude for the other person's positive actions and qualities. This reinforces positive behavior and fosters a supportive environment. Share in each other's successes and milestones. Celebrating together strengthens the emotional connection and creates lasting memories.

Set Healthy Boundaries

Clearly communicate your boundaries to others and respect theirs. Healthy boundaries prevent misunderstandings and ensure that everyone's needs are met. Allow others to have their own space and independence. Encourage each other to pursue individual interests and goals. Healthy boundaries act as a safeguard for your mental and emotional well-being. They prevent feelings of resentment, burnout, and overwhelm by ensuring that your needs are met and that you are not being taken advantage of. Boundaries help you manage your stress and maintain a balance between giving and receiving support. Setting boundaries is an act of self-respect. It shows that you value yourself enough to protect your energy, time, and emotional well-being. By defining and enforcing boundaries, you reinforce your self-worth and teach others to respect you. Without boundaries, you may find yourself overcommitted and overwhelmed, leading to physical and emotional exhaustion. Boundaries help you prioritize your well-being, work, and personal life, preventing burnout and promoting long-term productivity and happiness.

Resolve Conflicts Constructively

Don't let grievances fester. Address conflicts quickly and calmly to prevent them from escalating. If you feel you need to cool off prior to talking, meditate, take a walk, or have some alone time before returning to the conversation. Only you know what works best for you. Approach conflicts with the intention of finding mutually beneficial solutions. Focus on collaboration rather than competition. When you've made a mistake, offer a sincere apology. Similarly, practice forgiveness and letting go. This might be hard. Letting go is freedom to move on and grow in your journey of rekindling joy in your life. Here are some techniques you might try:

Stay Calm and Composed

It's important to manage your emotions during conflict. Taking deep breaths, pausing before responding, and remaining calm can prevent escalation and promote a constructive dialogue.

Seek Common Ground

Try to find areas of agreement or mutual interest that can serve as a foundation for resolving the conflict. Highlighting common goals can shift the focus from differences to collaboration.

Use a Problem-Solving Approach

Focus on a solution rather than dwelling on the problem. Brainstorm solutions together, evaluating the pros and cons of each option and agreeing on a mutually beneficial resolution.

Empathy and Understanding

There is a positive power to empathy in conflict resolution. Understanding the feelings and motivations of others can lead you to more compassionate responses and a deeper connection.

Set Boundaries

While resolving conflicts, it's crucial to establish healthy boundaries. Openly and clearly communicate your limits and respect those involved.

Follow Up

After a resolution, follow up to ensure the agreement is working well for everyone involved. This step is vital in reinforcing trust and preventing future conflicts.

There are many strategies for empowering relationships but try to approach conflicts as opportunities for growth and deeper understanding rather than mere hurdles. Employing these techniques not only leads to effective conflict resolution but also strengthens the relational bonds in your life.

Maintain a Positive Outlook

Focus on the positives in the relationship and in each other. Encourage and uplift one another whenever the opportunity arises. Share laughter and humor. Lighthearted moments can reduce stress and strengthen emotional connections. Nurturing supportive and positive relationships is a continuous practice. It's a lifelong process, but worth it. These relationships enrich your life, provide emotional support, and contribute to your overall well-being. Remember, as you are on this journey of rekindling joy, it's difficult to grow forward if you have unresolved conflicts in your life. Face them with strength and find resolutions.

ACTION ITEMS

List all your empowering relationships.

_____

_____

_____

_____

What relationships do not currently serve you in your quest for joy?

_____

_____

_____

_____

Write down three opportunities you are going to work on in building better communication to enrich your relationships. Give examples.

_____

_____

_____

_____

CHAPTER 12

THE IMPORTANCE OF CREATIVITY AND PLAY

C reativity is a powerful force that can significantly enhance joy and well-being for you. Engaging in creative activities allows for the expression of emotions, the exploration of new ideas, and the cultivation of a sense of achievement and fulfillment. Creativity provides a unique outlet for self-expression and exploration, which is essential for your emotional and mental well-being. Here's how creativity contributes to joy:

Creative Activities

Activities such as painting, writing, music, and dance allow you to express your emotions in a nonverbal way. This can be incredibly therapeutic, helping to release pent-up feelings and reduce stress. Engaging in creative pursuits encourages self-exploration. You can discover new aspects of your personality and potential, gaining a deeper understanding of yourself. This self-awareness fosters a sense of inner peace and joy. When was the last time you took the time to partake in a creative activity?

Mental Stimulation

Creativity stimulates your brain, enhancing cognitive function and promoting mental clarity. Creative activities often involve problem-solving and critical thinking, which can boost your cognitive flexibility and improve brain health. This mental stimulation keeps the mind sharp and engaged. Embracing creativity encourages innovative thinking and the ability to see the world from different perspectives. Creative activities are for every age.

Stress Relief and Relaxation

Engaging in creative activities is a natural stress reliever for you, providing a break from the demands of daily life. Many creative activities, such as drawing, knitting, and crossword puzzles require focused attention, which can promote mindfulness. This state of being in the present moment helps you reduce anxiety and induces relaxation. Creativity allows you to escape from your daily routines and immerse yourself in a world of imagination. This escape provides mental refreshment and rejuvenation, contributing to overall well-being and joy.

Sense of Accomplishment

Completing a creative project provides a sense of achievement and boosts self-esteem. Setting and reaching creative goals, whether it's finishing a painting, crafting, cooking a meal, or building something, fosters a sense of accomplishment. This boosts your confidence and reinforces your belief in your abilities. It does not need to be a big, time-consuming project. Creating something unique brings a sense of pride and joy. Sharing these creations with others can further enhance these feelings and create a sense of connection and validation.

Building Community and Connections

Creative activities often bring people together, fostering a sense of community and connection. Participating in group creative projects or workshops encourages collaboration and the sharing of ideas. This sense of teamwork can build strong bonds and enhance social support networks. This creates a sense of belonging.

Creativity is a vital contributor to joy for all of us. It offers you a unique outlet for self-expression, mental stimulation, stress relief, a sense of accomplishment, community building, and the enhancement of everyday life. By embracing creativity, you can foster a greater sense of well-being, resilience, and fulfillment, leading to a more joyful and enriched life.

The Why for Engaging in Group Fitness and Wellness Activities

Engaging in group fitness and wellness activities offers numerous benefits that extend beyond physical health. Group fitness provides a supportive and motivating environment that fosters both personal and communal well-being. Here's why you should consider participating in group fitness and wellness activities:

Social Connection and Support

One of the most significant benefits of group fitness is the opportunity to connect with like-minded individuals. In a group setting, you can build a sense of community and camaraderie. Group activities create a social environment where you can meet new friends and strengthen existing relationships. This social engagement can reduce feelings of isolation and loneliness. Working out with others who share similar fitness goals can be incredibly motivating. The collective support and encouragement help maintain commitment and enthusiasm. Having a workout buddy or being part of a group increases accountability. It's harder to skip a workout when you know others are counting on you to show up. Group fitness classes often come with a built-in support system that can significantly boost motivation and keep you engaged. Consider joining a walking, hiking, or cycling group. The energy of a group workout can be invigorating. The collective effort and shared experience create a positive environment that makes workouts more enjoyable. Lighthearted competition within a group can spur you to improve your performance and achieve your fitness goals faster.

Variety and Fun

Group fitness classes offer a range of activities, from yoga and Pilates to dance classes and high-intensity interval training (HIIT). This variety keeps workouts interesting and fun. Trying different classes can help you discover new interests and passions that you may not have considered before. Group fitness is designed to be enjoyable, often combining music, choreography, and social interaction, making exercise feel more like a fun activity than a chore. Regular participation in group fitness activities offers physical- and mental-health benefits; empowerment; and confidence, which leads to higher self-esteem and joy. Group fitness classes often involve learning new skills and techniques, contributing to personal growth. From mastering a yoga pose to perfecting dance moves, group fitness classes offer you opportunities to learn and improve. Regular attendance at fitness classes fosters discipline and the development of healthy habits that extend beyond the gym.

Engaging in group fitness and wellness activities offers numerous benefits for you. These include social connection, increased motivation, variety, fun, enhanced physical and mental health, empowerment, and learning opportunities. Participating in group fitness can lead you to a more enjoyable and sustainable fitness journey, fostering a supportive community and promoting overall well-being.

Achieving Goals

Setting and achieving fitness goals within a supportive group fosters a sense of accomplishment and self-efficacy. Group fitness promotes body positivity by focusing on health and strength over appearance. This can lead you to a healthier self-image and greater body confidence. Overcoming physical challenges in a group setting reinforces the belief that you are strong, capable, and resilient.

Fun and Spontaneous Ways for You to Stay Active and Joyful

Staying active doesn't have to be a chore. Incorporating fun and spontaneous activities into your routine can bring joy, energy, and a sense of adventure to your life. Here are some enjoyable and unplanned ways for you to stay active and develop joy.

Dance like no one's watching! Dancing is a fantastic way (my favorite) to get your heart rate up and release those feel-good endorphins. Turn up your favorite music and have a dance party in your living room. You can be the only attendee. Let loose and move to the rhythm without worrying about how you look. It's a great way to burn calories and lift your spirits. In fact, sometimes I get out of bed, turn on the music, and just start dancing. It's a great way to start your day!

Try a group dance class like Zumba, hip-hop, or salsa. These classes are designed to be fun and energetic, making exercise feel like a celebration.

Head to a nearby park, forest, or hiking trail. The beauty of nature can make physical activity feel less like exercise and more like an adventure. Invite your friends or family to join you for added fun. If you live near a beach, take advantage of the sand and surf. Activities like beach volleyball, paddleboarding, or simply walking along the shoreline can be incredibly enjoyable and physically engaging.

Turn cleaning or gardening into a workout. Play upbeat music and add extra movements like lunges or squats as you tidy up. It's productive and keeps you active.

Embrace your inner child with playful activities that are both fun and physically engaging. Engage in casual sports and games that don't require a lot of planning. Join or organize pickup games of basketball, soccer, pickleball, or Frisbee. These spontaneous games are energetic and enjoyable ways to stay active.

Make physical activity a social event by involving friends and family. Plan group outings that involve physical activity, such as hiking trips, dance parties, or yoga sessions in the park. Drag a friend to a new fitness class. Sharing the experience makes it more enjoyable and provides mutual encouragement.

Bottom line: Staying active and joyful can be achieved through a variety of fun and spontaneous activities. Whether it's dancing, exploring the outdoors, playing like a kid, joining casual sports, incorporating movement into daily life, trying new things, or socializing with active friends, the key is to find activities that bring joy and excitement. By integrating these playful and unstructured forms of exercise into your routine, you can maintain a healthy and vibrant lifestyle filled with laughter, spontaneity, and joy.

ACTION ITEMS

List three creative activities that you currently do on a regular basis.

_____

_____

_____

_____

Write down three to five creative activities you would enjoy trying but haven't taken the time for. Circle one and schedule it on your calendar.

_____

_____

_____

_____

What movements can you incorporate with ease into your daily life?

_____

_____

_____

_____

List three activities you can incorporate in your life involving your family and friends.

_____

_____

_____

_____

CHAPTER 13

PRACTICING GRATITUDE

The Science and Benefits of Practicing Gratitude

I have discussed gratitude many times in this book. It is very important for your journey to understand it more deeply. Gratitude is more than just a fleeting feeling; it is a powerful practice that can significantly enhance overall well-being. Gratitude invites you to shift your perspective from focusing on what is lacking in your life to appreciating the abundance of blessings that surround you. By recognizing and appreciating the positive aspects of life, we can improve our mental, emotional, and even physical health. Juliana Breines wrote an article for *Greater Good Magazine* titled "Four Great Gratitude Strategies."[xv] In it, several gratitude experts discuss their research on the positive outcomes of practicing gratitude. We know that when we start the day with gratitude, our disposition is improved. You can be in bed or having coffee and also practice gratitude. Just start the day with gratitude. Also, end the day with gratitude. Just this little shift to reflecting on all the things you are thankful for can bring joy into your soul. Cultivate a sense of gratitude for the small blessings in your life. Take time each day to reflect on the things you are thankful for, whether it's a warm cup of tea, a kind gesture from a friend, or a beautiful sunset. Gratitude can shift your focus toward joy. By cultivating a mindset of gratitude, you can unlock the hidden blessings in your daily experiences, foster deeper connections with others, and cultivate a sense of contentment and fulfillment that transcends challenges and difficulties. By acknowledging and expressing gratitude for the simple pleasures, moments of joy, and acts of kindness that you encounter each day, you can cultivate a sense of richness and fulfillment that transcends material possessions. Gratitude is a powerful emotion that can transform you by shifting your focus from what's lacking to appreciating what you have. Developing gratitude skills is a journey that involves altering your mindset and habits. Here are some tips to develop gratitude skills:

Start a Gratitude Journal

Keep a gratitude journal where you can write down three things you are grateful for each day. This practice helps in recognizing positive aspects of your life and promotes a habit of appreciation. Writing regularly can deepen awareness of daily blessings, big or small, and create a repository of positivity you can revisit during challenging times.

Practice Mindful Gratitude

Mindfulness and gratitude go hand in hand. Practice being fully present in the moment and acknowledge the good that surrounds you. Whether it's savoring a meal, enjoying nature, or spending time with loved ones, mindful awareness opens the door to deeper appreciation and contentment.

Express Gratitude to Others

Cultivating gratitude also involves expressing it. Write thank you notes or verbally express appreciation to the people in your life. This strengthens your relationships, fosters connection, and encourages a cycle of positive interaction. Practicing verbal gratitude can create a ripple effect, spreading kindness and appreciation throughout your community.

Reflect on Challenges

Gratitude isn't limited to good times; it also involves recognizing the growth that arises from adversity. Take the time to reflect on past challenges and identify lessons learned or strengths gained. This practice nurtures resilience and helps shift your perspective from viewing difficulties as setbacks to seeing them as opportunities for growth and gratitude.

Visualize What Could Be Different

Imagine life without certain comforts or people. This technique can highlight the importance of things you might otherwise take for granted and renew appreciation for their presence.

Incorporate Gratitude into Routines

Start integrating gratitude into daily routines, such as during morning or evening rituals. Starting or ending the day with gratitude can set a positive tone and improve overall mindset.

Consistency is key, even if you spend just a few moments each day reflecting on what you are grateful for.

Embrace the Small Stuff

Be watchful and appreciate the small joys. From enjoying a good cup of coffee to experiencing a sunny day, acknowledging simple pleasures can have a positive cumulative effect on your outlook.

Gratitude is a skill that requires practice but can become a natural, uplifting part of daily life. By incorporating gratitude techniques, you can develop a more grateful mindset, leading to greater happiness, stronger relationships, and a more fulfilled existence. I encourage you to take small, consistent steps, and soon you will discover the transformative power of gratitude in your life.

Gratitude acts as a magnet for joy, attracting more positive experiences and emotions into your life. It deepens your connections with others and fosters a sense of appreciation and reciprocity in your relationships. By expressing gratitude toward friends, family members, colleagues, and strangers, you will strengthen bonds, build trust, and create a supportive network of love and kindness that enriches your life and the lives of those around you.

Gratitude serves as a source of strength and resilience during challenging times. When you practice gratitude in the face of adversity, you cultivate a sense of hope, optimism, and inner courage that helps you navigate difficulties with grace and courage. Gratitude empowers you to find silver linings, lessons, and blessings, even in the midst of hardship.

It has a major impact on your physical and mental well-being. Research has shown that practicing gratitude can reduce stress, improve sleep quality, boost immune function, lower blood pressure, and enhance overall health. By practicing gratitude, you nurture your mind-body connection and promote holistic well-being.

Cultivation of Abundance

Gratitude opens the door to abundance and prosperity by shifting your focus from scarcity to sufficiency. When we appreciate the blessings, opportunities, and resources available to us, we attract more abundance into our lives and create a sense of prosperity that transcends material wealth. Gratitude is a magnet for abundance and fulfillment.

Cultivating Presence

Gratitude invites you to be present in the moment and savor the beauty and wonder of life. By cultivating a sense of gratitude for the here and now, you deepen your connection to the present moment, heighten your awareness of the blessings that surround you, and experience a profound sense of peace and fulfillment. I have gratitude cards in my purse and in my car. I leave them behind for individuals who have shown me kindness in a restaurant or a store. If I have the chance to observe them when they open the card, the joy I receive is priceless.

Gratitude inspires acts of generosity and kindness toward others. When we express gratitude, we are more inclined to pay it forward, share our blessings, and contribute to the well-being of others. The practice fuels a cycle of giving and receiving that enriches our lives and the lives of those we touch. This is a life-changing practice that has the power to elevate your well-being, foster joy, abundance, strengthen relationships, build resilience, and cultivate a sense of fulfillment and contentment. By embracing gratitude as a daily practice, you can shift your perspective. You will amplify your joy, deepen your connections, and create a ripple effect of positivity and kindness that enriches your life and the lives around you. Embrace the power of gratitude, and watch as your heart expands with love, appreciation, and joy for the blessings that surround you.

ACTION ITEMS

Start a gratitude journal today.

_____

_____

_____

_____

In the next five minutes, write down everything you are grateful for in your life right now!

_____

_____

_____

_____

Send a text or email to someone today expressing gratitude to them. This can be just one or two lines. Try to do this a few times a week. Watch for the response, but more importantly, be cognizant of how it makes you feel.

_____

_____

_____

_____

Start and end each day with gratitude, morning and evening. Take one to three minutes to focus on your blessings.

_____

_____

_____

_____

Start a gratitude jar. This can be as simple as a mason jar. Each day drop at least one note of gratitude into it. It is a wonderful reminder for you.

_____

_____

_____

_____

CHAPTER 14

LIVING A BALANCED LIFE

L iving a balanced life is essential for maintaining joy and overall well-being, especially for those of us who juggle multiple roles and responsibilities. Striking a balance between various aspects of life—from work and family to personal interests and self-care—can lead us to enhanced mental, emotional, and physical health. Living a balanced life is not just for the wealthy. In fact, I have taken care of many wealthy patients who were very out of balance. And often, once you think you are living a balanced life, life throws you curve balls. It's OK. We just re-evaluate how to adjust and reset. Here's why balance is vital for us to sustain joy and how it contributes to a fulfilling life:

Prevents Burnout

Balance plays a crucial role in preventing burnout. We frequently manage a multitude of commitments, including career, household duties, childcare, and social obligations. Without balance, this constant juggling can lead us to physical and emotional exhaustion.

Sustainability

Balance ensures that efforts are sustainable over the long-term. By allocating time and energy wisely, we can avoid the debilitating effects of burnout and maintain our productivity and enthusiasm. Incorporating rest and relaxation into one's routine allows for recovery and rejuvenation. This renewed energy is vital for approaching our daily tasks with a positive and joyful mindset.

Enhancing Mental and Emotional Health

Mental health is significantly impacted by the balance we maintain in our lives. Overemphasis on any single area can lead to stress, anxiety, and a sense of overwhelm. Achieving balance helps reduce your stress by ensuring that no single aspect of life dominates at the expense of others. This harmonious approach promotes a calm and stable mental state. Balance contributes to emotional stability by fostering a sense of control and predictability in one's life. When we feel balanced, we are better equipped to handle emotional challenges and maintain a positive outlook.

Fostering Personal Growth

Finding balance allows you to engage in activities that promote personal growth and development. Focusing solely on career or family can lead us to neglect personal interests and passions. Leading a life filled with balance encourages us to pursue diverse interests, whether it's enjoying a hobby, learning a new skill, or engaging in creative activities. These pursuits contribute to a richer, more satisfying life experience. Allocating time for personal interests fosters continuous learning and self-improvement, which are integral to personal growth, fulfillment, and joy.

Strengthening Relationships

Relationships are a cornerstone for your joy and well-being. Maintaining balance ensures that you have the time and energy to nurture your relationships with family, friends, and partner. Balanced living allows for meaningful quality time with loved ones. This strengthens bonds, fosters mutual support, and enhances happiness. When you are not overwhelmed by an imbalanced life, you can communicate more effectively and empathetically, leading to healthier and more fulfilling relationships.

Promoting Physical Health

Physical health is intricately linked to balance. Research by Andrea Gragnano and colleagues in 2020 emphasized the benefits of work-life balance, highlighting that individuals who managed to balance work demands with personal life tended to experience less stress and related health problems, such as hypertension and cardiovascular issues.[xvi] A life dominated by work or stress can lead to neglecting essential health practices. Regular physical activity, a nutritious diet, and adequate sleep are part of balance; all are crucial for maintaining physical health and vitality. By avoiding overexertion and stress, a balanced lifestyle helps prevent various health issues, such as cardiovascular disease, obesity, and chronic fatigue.

Cultivating Joy and Fulfillment

Ultimately, balance is vital for cultivating a sense of joy and fulfillment. When we achieve balance, we create a life that aligns with our values and priorities. This fosters inner peace and contentment. When all areas of life are in harmony, we can experience a deep sense of satisfaction and joy. Balance allows us to fulfill our roles and responsibilities while also prioritizing our own happiness and well-being. This holistic approach ensures a more joyful and enriched life.

Finding and maintaining our balance is essential for sustaining joy and overall well-being. By preventing burnout, enhancing mental health, fostering personal growth, strengthening relationships, promoting physical health, and cultivating joy and fulfillment, balance contributes significantly to a rich and satisfying life. Prioritizing balance enables you to navigate the complexities of modern life with grace, resilience, and positivity, leading to lasting happiness and a deeper sense of purpose.

Here are some tips for finding balance in your world. I know it seems long and overwhelming, but don't get stressed out. Start by trying to incorporate two of the following ideas and see how they work for you.

Set Clear Boundaries

Define specific times for work and personal activities. Then, communicate these boundaries to family, friends, and colleagues. I highly suggest a family calendar that's visible to everyone. This can be a digital calendar or a traditional paper one, maybe in the kitchen or a common area. Be specific on the calendar about different priorities at different times, possibly in different colors. Make it a fun experience for all!

Prioritize Tasks

Make sure to differentiate on your calendar between urgent or important tasks and fun creative time. This will help you see if your routine is in balance. Really take a hard look at what truly matters to you, both at work and at home. Do you feel you are balancing work and personal time appropriately for success and fulfillment?

Learn to Say No

I know it's hard, but you must recognize your limits and the importance of declining additional responsibilities that may compromise your balance. This is hard for many of us, but very crucial for aiming toward a balanced life.

Focus on Self-Care

Schedule consistent self-care practices, including exercise, meditation, and hobbies, on your calendar to maintain physical and mental health. Remember to include family and friends in certain activities. It's a win for all.

Foster Supportive Relationships

Recognize the value of building a strong support network with family, friends, and colleagues who understand and respect your need for balance. Everyone is trying to find balance in their life. Honestly, it's a great conversation to start with your support community. I am sure you will pick up some pearls that might work in your home. You are not alone. All of us are trying to figure out the balance that works for us.

Regular Reflection

Take the time for journaling or regular reflection on how your balanced life is going, make adjustments in areas needing attention, and most of all, celebrate successes. Don't forget to celebrate small wins like getting to the grocery store to buy ingredients for cooking dinner, making it out for a ten-minute walk, and having time to read to your children at bedtime.

Schedule Regular Breaks and Vacations

Always plan time for regular breaks throughout the day. Enjoy planning day trips and larger vacations to recharge and maintain enthusiasm in both areas of life. These do not need to be elaborate or expensive. Take a walk, have lunch in a park, watch a movie, or plan a trip you can afford. What's important is that you make time for you and your community of people.

Finding Joy in a Spiritual Journey

The quest for joy is a universal pursuit that crosses all cultures, languages, and personal experiences. At its core joy is deeply rooted in our inner beings and often linked to a genuine spiritual connection. In the pursuit of personal growth and self-improvement, many people focus on developing their skills, setting goals, and improving their physical health. While these aspects are crucial, having a spiritual connection is equally important for becoming the best version of yourself.

Spirituality provides a deeper meaning and purpose to life. It allows you to connect with something greater than yourself, whether that is a higher power, nature, or the universe. This connection can bring a sense of peace, fulfillment, and inner strength that can help you navigate life's challenges with resilience and grace. Having a spiritual connection also fosters a sense of gratitude and appreciation for the present moment. It encourages you to be mindful, to be fully present and engaged in your experiences, and to find joy in the simple things in life. It can also provide a moral compass, guiding you to make ethical decisions and act with compassion and empathy toward others. It encourages kindness, forgiveness, and understanding, fostering harmonious relationships and a sense of unity with the world around us. Spirituality involves the recognition of a reality greater than our sensory experiences. It's about perceiving a deeper meaning and purpose in life, which often leads to a connection with a higher power or universal energy. This connection nurtures your inner life and profoundly influences your outer life, including your capacity to experience joy.

The key element of spiritual connection is that it offers a sense of belonging and purpose. When you feel connected to something greater than yourself, it provides a framework within which you can understand your existence and place in the world. This sense of purpose and belonging brings profound joy because it satisfies your intrinsic need for meaning and connection.

Just as important, spirituality fosters compassion and love, both for yourself and for others. This compassionate outlook on life creates meaningful relationships and connections, which are essential for your joy. When you feel connected to others through love and compassion, your life is enriched, and you will experience a deep, abiding joy. The resilience that comes from a spiritual connection cannot be overstated. Life inevitably brings challenges and hardships, but a strong spiritual foundation helps you navigate these difficulties with grace and strength. By trusting in a higher power or the wisdom of the universe, you can find joy even in difficult times, knowing that you are supported and that there is a greater purpose to your journey.

A spiritual connection brings a sense of purpose, peace, gratitude, compassion, and resilience, all of which contribute to a joyous life. By nurturing your spiritual self, you cultivate an inner wellspring of joy that can sustain you through life's ups and downs. Embracing spirituality in whatever form resonates with you personally can lead to a life filled with deeper, more enduring joy. Having a spiritual connection can enhance creativity and intuition. It opens the door to inspiration, insight, and innovation, allowing you to tap into your inner wisdom and unleash your creative potential. This creative flow can lead to breakthroughs, new ideas, and innovative solutions to challenges. Overall, integrating spirituality into your life is essential for holistic growth and well-being. It nurtures the mind, body, and soul, creating a sense of balance, harmony, and wholeness. By cultivating a spiritual connection, you can unlock your potential, live authentically, and enrich your life with joy and more meaning.

The Connection Between Joy, Health, Lifestyle, and Lifespan

The connection between joy, health, lifestyle, and lifespan is a fascinating and important topic. When we are happy, our bodies release endorphins and other feel-good hormones that can boost our immune system, reduce stress levels, and even lower blood pressure. The relationship is profound. The relationship between the four has a significant impact on your emotional well-being, physical health, and longevity. Health span refers to the period of life spent in good health, free from chronic diseases and disabilities, and is influenced by various factors, including lifestyle choices, genetics, and environmental factors, just to name a few.

Happiness and joy play a crucial role in promoting an extended health span by positively influencing both mental and physical well-being.

Research has shown that those of us who experience high levels of happiness and joy tend to have better overall health outcomes and a longer health span. Researchers Jingping Xu and Robert E. Roberts found that happiness and positive mental health can predict reductions in diseases such as heart disease and diabetes, indicating that joyful individuals may experience fewer chronic health conditions.[xvii] Positive emotions can boost your immune system, reduce inflammation, lower stress levels, and improve cardiovascular health. By cultivating a positive mindset and nurturing feelings of happiness and joy, you can enhance your resilience to illness and improve your overall quality of life.

Happiness and joy act as powerful antidotes to stress, which is a significant contributor to various chronic conditions and premature aging. When we experience positive emotions, such as laughter, gratitude, and contentment, the body releases many feel-good hormones, like endorphins and oxytocin, which help reduce stress and promote relaxation. By managing your stress effectively through the cultivation of happiness and joy, you can enhance your resilience to adversity and maintain an optimal health span.

Positive emotions like happiness and joy are often intertwined with social connections and support systems, which play a vital role in promoting health span. Strong social ties and meaningful relationships have been linked to improved mental health, reduced risk of chronic diseases, and increased longevity. The Harvard Study of Adult Development, begun in 1938, found a clear link between close relationships and longer, healthier lives.[xviii] Good relationships were found to protect not only physical health but also mental well-being as people age. By fostering positive relationships and engaging in activities that bring joy and fulfillment, we can create a supportive network that contributes to our overall well-being and health span.

When you strive to be the best version of yourself, you are not only enhancing your quality of life in the present moment but also setting the stage for a long, healthy lifespan. By prioritizing personal growth, self-care, and authenticity, you create a foundation for well-being that supports your physical, mental, and emotional health. Healthy lifestyle choices can reduce the risk of chronic diseases such as heart disease, diabetes, and obesity, and promote overall vitality and longevity. By practicing self-care, mindfulness, and stress management, you can reduce the risk of mental health conditions such as anxiety and depression. You can also enhance your cognitive function, mood regulation, and overall mental well-being. By nurturing positive relationships, setting boundaries, and expressing your true self, you can create a supportive environment that fosters emotional well-being and longevity. By pursuing activities that bring you joy, fulfillment, and a sense of contribution, you can enhance your overall well-being, satisfaction, and longevity. Having a sense of purpose has been linked to increased longevity and a higher quality of life. When you live as the best version of yourself, you are more likely to experience a higher quality of life characterized by vitality, resilience, and a sense of fulfillment. By prioritizing self-care, personal growth, and positive relationships, you can create a life that is vibrant, balanced, meaningful, enhancing your overall well-being and longevity.

The Importance of Diet, Exercise, and Overall Wellness for Finding and Maintaining Joy

Nourishing Body and Soul

A balanced and nutritious diet is fundamental to overall wellness and joy. We all know this. What we eat has a direct impact on our physical health, mental clarity, and emotional stability. Consuming a diet rich in whole foods such as fruits, vegetables, lean proteins, whole grains, and healthy fats provides us with the essential nutrients that fuel our body. Macronutrients (proteins, fats, and carbohydrates) and micronutrients (vitamins and minerals) are vital for optimal bodily functions. Certain nutrients, like omega-3 fatty acids (found in fish, flaxseeds, and walnuts), are crucial for brain health and can improve your mood and cognitive function. Foods rich in antioxidants, like berries and dark leafy greens, combat oxidative stress, which can reduce the risk of depression and anxiety.

Eating a well-balanced diet can help you maintain steady energy levels throughout the day. Avoiding processed foods and high-sugar snacks helps prevent energy crashes and maintain stable blood sugar levels, contributing to overall vitality and mood stability. An article by nutritionist Dr. Shilpa Thakur states that the food you choose has a significant impact on your energy levels and productivity.[xix] She discusses how to feed your body and brain with a balanced diet and avoid the blood sugar roller coaster. Research her work. You will find it very interesting.

The gut-brain connection highlights the importance of gut health for mental well-being. Probiotic-rich foods like yogurt, kimchi, and sauerkraut promote healthy gut flora, which is linked to better mood and reduced symptoms of depression. There is a lot of research being done on the importance of good gut health. Understanding the gut-mind connection is fascinating and one of the hottest topics in medicine. Research keeps uncovering more information about this important connection.[xx] The relationship between our gut and mind, often referred to as the gut-brain axis, underscores the profound impact our digestive system has on mental health and vice versa. This bidirectional communication pathway is complex and influenced by numerous factors including diet, stress, and gut microbiome. The gut-brain axis involves direct and indirect pathways linking cognitive and emotional centers of the brain with peripheral intestinal functions. This connection is mainly facilitated through but not limited to:

Neural Pathways

The vagus nerve plays a critical role in transmitting signals between the gut and the brain. It helps regulate gut motility and communicates feelings of satiety and wellness to the brain.

Chemical Messaging

Neurotransmitters, such as serotonin, are produced in the gut and influence mood and cognitive function. An estimated 90–95 percent of serotonin is synthesized in the gastrointestinal tract,[xxi] highlighting its significance.

Immune System

Both the gut and the brain are integral parts of the body's immune response. Gut health can significantly influence systemic inflammation, impacting mental health conditions like depression and anxiety.

Gut Microbiota/Microbiome

The trillions of bacteria residing in the gut have a significant role. They produce metabolites that can alter brain function and behavior, emphasizing the importance of a balanced microbiome.

Impact on Mental Health

Research indicates that an imbalance in gut bacteria, known as dysbiosis, is linked to numerous mental health disorders. Conditions such as anxiety, depression, and even neurodegenerative diseases have been shown to be correlated with gut health.[xxii]

Mood Regulation

Probiotics and a diet rich in fiber can promote beneficial bacteria growth, potentially reducing symptoms of depression and anxiety.

Cognitive Function

A healthy gut microbiome is believed to support cognitive function and may influence the development or progression of neurodegenerative disorders.

Stress Resilience

The gut can impact how the body responds to stressors, potentially enhancing resilience through a balanced diet and stress management practices.

Here are some tips on how to support a healthy gut-brain axis:

Balanced Nutrition

Incorporate a diet rich in whole foods, prebiotics, and probiotics to promote a flourishing microbiome. Whole food diets are ones that revolve around foods in their natural form: fresh fruits and vegetables, whole grains like brown rice, lean proteins, nuts, seeds, olive oil, and legumes. These are just the start of a diet rich in whole foods. Make it easy for yourself. Pick a few of these and build some simple dinners around the above items. Nuts and seeds make a great nutritious snack.

Stress Management

Incorporating regular exercise, mindfulness, and adequate sleep can enhance your gut health and reduce stress.

Mindful Eating

Pay attention to how your food impacts your mood and energy. This can guide you to better dietary choices.

In conclusion, nurturing the gut-mind connection is essential for overall well-being. By adopting healthy lifestyle choices, we can influence this powerful axis to improve both mental and physical health outcomes. I will give you some ideas for this in the Action Items section.

Exercise

Regular physical activity is a cornerstone of a joyful and healthy life. Exercise offers a multitude of benefits that extend far beyond physical fitness. We have already discussed this in depth. Engaging in regular exercise strengthens the cardiovascular system, builds muscle, enhances flexibility, and promotes bone density. These physical benefits contribute to overall longevity and quality of life. Exercise is a natural mood booster. Physical activity stimulates the release of neurotransmitters like endorphins, serotonin, and dopamine, which enhance mood and reduce stress levels. This natural high can alleviate symptoms of depression and anxiety, promoting mental well-being.

A Holistic Approach to Joy

Wellness is an important foundation upon which joy and fulfillment are built. It encompasses the balance of physical health, mental clarity, emotional stability, and spiritual alignment. Adequate sleep is crucial for overall wellness. Quality sleep allows the body to repair itself, supports cognitive function, and regulates mood. Developing a regular sleep routine and prioritizing rest can dramatically improve your well-being.

Practices like mindfulness meditation, deep breathing exercises, and progressive muscle relaxation help manage stress and promote mental clarity. Taking time for self-care activities, such as reading, soaking in a bath, or pursuing hobbies, can also enhance emotional well-being.

Building and maintaining strong social connections is integral to wellness. Positive relationships provide emotional support, reduce feelings of loneliness, and enhance life satisfaction. Engaging in social activities, whether with family, friends, or community groups, reinforces a sense of belonging and joy. Finding and pursuing passions and a sense of purpose can significantly enhance overall wellness. Engaging in activities that resonate with one's values and interests brings fulfillment and a sense of meaning to life.

To truly find and maintain joy, it's essential to integrate diet, exercise, and wellness into a cohesive lifestyle framework. Dedicate time for meal planning and preparation. Focus on incorporating a variety of whole foods that work for you and your family, and minimize processed items. I know this is hard when children see commercials on television for fast food restaurants. Also, what they see other children eating at school is not always healthy. Take the time to be present to listen to your body's hunger signals and eat mindfully. Prioritize physical activity by scheduling it into your daily routine. Choose activities that you enjoy and that align with your fitness level and goals. Consistency is key to reaping the benefits of exercise. Develop daily habits that promote your overall wellness. This includes adequate sleep, hydration, stress management, limiting alcohol and other recreational drugs, and fostering social connections. Create a balance that allows for personal growth, relaxation, and social engagement. I urge you to make yourself a calendar and schedule your meals (that are healthy for everyone), family time, personal time, and professional time. It's not easy but achievable. Make it simple. We all know what we should be doing, but actually doing these things is a different story for many of us. Use your calendar as your visual. I used to involve my family in developing the menus for the week. I set parameters for the different menus and foods, and we developed our meal plan for the week together. I wanted everyone to learn and to feel they had input on the family meals. I made it fun!

The Power of Positive Thinking

Positive thinking is more than just a mindset. It's a way of life that can profoundly impact your well-being, resilience, and longevity. Having a positive outlook involves being in the present. By cultivating optimism and a positive outlook on life, you can enhance your mental and physical health, improve your relationships, and navigate life's challenges with grace and resilience. Positive thinking involves maintaining a hopeful and optimistic attitude toward life, even in the face of adversity. It's about focusing on the good, finding silver linings in difficult situations, and approaching life with a sense of gratitude and resilience. When you choose to embrace a positive mindset, you open yourself up to a world of possibilities and opportunities. Positivity is not just about having a sunny outlook on life, it is a mindset that can shape your thoughts, actions, and ultimately, your reality.

One of the key benefits of cultivating positivity in your life is the impact it has on your mental and emotional well-being. When we focus on the positive aspects of our lives, we are better able to manage stress, anxiety, and other negative emotions. Positivity helps us build resilience and cope with challenges more effectively, leading to greater overall happiness and fulfillment.

Moreover, positivity has a ripple effect on our relationships with others. When we approach interactions with a positive attitude, we are more likely to attract like-minded individuals and foster strong, supportive connections. Positivity can enhance communication, build trust, and create a sense of unity and collaboration in both personal and professional relationships. Positivity can fuel your personal growth and development. When you believe in yourself and your abilities, you are more likely to take risks, pursue your goals, and overcome obstacles. Positivity encourages you to step out of your comfort zone, embrace change, and seize opportunities for growth and learning.

Positivity can have a profound impact on your physical health. Research has shown that maintaining a positive outlook can boost your immune system, lower stress levels, and even increase your lifespan.[xxiii]

So embrace the power of positivity in your life. Cultivate a mindset of optimism, gratitude, and resilience. Choose to see the good in every situation and watch as your life unfolds in ways you never thought possible. Remember, positivity is not just a mindset. It's a superpower that can help you create the life of your dreams. Here are some practical steps to guide you in developing positive thinking:

Practice Gratitude

Count your blessings by maintaining a gratitude journal. Writing down three things you are grateful for each day can shift your focus from what's lacking to appreciating the abundance in your life.

Challenge Negative Thoughts

Become aware of negative thought patterns. When faced with pessimistic thoughts, you should challenge their validity and restructure them into more positive, realistic thinking. This can be done through the cognitive restructuring techniques that we discussed earlier in the book.

Visualize Success

Visualization can be a powerful tool. Regularly envision successful outcomes in your personal and professional life, no matter how small or big. Visualization helps instill confidence and prepares your mind to handle real-life situations positively.

Surround Yourself with Positivity

Your environment significantly influences your mindset. Seek out positive relationships and environments that uplift you, minimizing exposure to negativity wherever possible.

Mindfulness and Meditation

Practicing mindfulness helps you stay present and aware, reducing the impact of negative thoughts. Daily meditation can promote a calm and centered mindset, enabling positive thinking.

Affirmations

Use positive affirmations to boost your self-esteem and outlook. Affirmations, repeated consistently, can rewire thinking patterns by reinforcing positive beliefs about yourself.

Take Care of Physical Health

Don't forget the important connection between physical well-being and mental positivity. Regular exercise, a balanced diet, and sufficient sleep can make a significant difference in your mood and energy levels.

Learn from Challenges

Encourage a mindset that views challenges as opportunities for growth rather than setbacks. View adversity as a challenge to foster resilience and optimism.

Developing positivity is a process that takes time and effort. Be patient with yourself, practice self-compassion, and embrace the power of positivity to transform your life in meaningful ways. By incorporating strategies for positivity into your daily routine, you can cultivate a mindset of optimism, resilience, and joy that will empower you to navigate life's challenges with grace and positivity. Remember, rekindling your joy is a journey, and it's OK to have ups and downs along the way. Be patient and kind with yourself as you explore what brings you joy and make it a priority in your life. Embrace the process and celebrate the moments of joy, no matter how small. Your happiness and well-being are worth it!

ACTION ITEMS

List three steps you can take today in each category below to find more balance.

Self

_____

_____

_____

Family

_____

_____

_____

Relationships

_____

_____

_____

Career

_____

_____

_____

Think about your current day-to-day activities. What can you say "no" to immediately?

_____

_____

_____

_____

Make a list of whole foods, seeds, and whole grains. Google simple recipes to incorporate whole foods. Take a look at your family's favorite menus and see where you can substitute healthy alternatives. Make a list of three to five meals that you will have in the coming week. Put them on the calendar or in a place where everyone can see them easily.

_____

_____

_____

_____

IMPORTANT—Designate a calendar for the home where you will show priorities, activities and meals for you and the family. This is a great way to get more balance in your life and stimulate communication within the home.

CHAPTER 15

~

COMMUNITY AND SERVICE

Finding Joy Through Community:
The Power of Belonging

In the pursuit of joy and fulfillment, the power of community cannot be underestimated. Being part of a supportive network not only enriches our lives but also enhances our overall well-being. Communities offer spaces where you can connect, share experiences, and collaborate, ultimately leading to a profound sense of belonging and happiness. But how can you find the right community? Here are some actionable steps to guide you on this journey:

First, understand the importance of identifying your interests and passions. Communities are often formed around shared hobbies, causes, or goals, so knowing what sparks joy and curiosity for you is a crucial first step. Think about activities you enjoy, whether they involve art, sports, volunteering, or learning a new skill. This reflection will serve as a guiding light in your search for like-minded individuals.

Next, explore both local and online opportunities. Local communities can be found through community centers, libraries, or local events. I suggest checking bulletin boards or community newsletters for clubs and gatherings. Online platforms, on the other hand, provide broader reach. Social media platforms like Instagram, Facebook Groups, and other specialized forums can connect you with global communities aligned with your interests.

You will need to take the initiative to attend gatherings or join online discussions. Participation is key to feeling connected. Even though stepping into a new group can be daunting, community members are often welcoming and eager to share their passions with you. Start with small events or introductory sessions to ease into the community.

A strong sense of belonging is fundamental to human happiness. Being part of a community creates an environment where you feel included, accepted, and valued. Knowing that you are part of a community provides emotional security and a sense of stability. This support system can provide a buffer against feelings of loneliness and isolation, enhancing overall mental health. Communities often form around shared interests, values, or goals. This common ground fosters a sense of identity and belonging, which is critical for self-esteem and emotional well-being.

I urge you to expose yourself to diversity and adopt an openness to new experiences. Seek out communities that offer fresh perspectives and new friendships. Exploring different cultures, ideas, and traditions within a community can not only broaden your horizons but also deepen your personal joy. It's important to nurture existing relationships within communities. Consistent engagement and communication are essential for building lasting bonds. Be an active participant by offering your skills, supporting other members, or organizing events. Finding joy in community is a personal journey. The path might include trial and error to discover where you truly feel at home. I wish you patience and persistence, as finding the right fit can take time, but the rewards of belonging to a community are immeasurable.

Opportunities for Social Interaction

Regular social interaction is vital for your mental health and happiness. Being part of a community provides you with ample opportunities for meaningful connections. Communities foster friendship and connection. Regular interaction with community members can lead you to deep, lasting relationships that enrich life. Being active in a community can expand your social network, opening doors to new opportunities and experiences. Networking within a supportive community can enhance your personal and professional growth.

Enhancing Purpose and Meaning

Being part of a community can provide you with a strong sense of purpose and meaning, which are essential for long-term happiness. Communities often unite around common causes or goals. Contributing to these collective efforts can give you a sense of purpose and the satisfaction of making a difference. Active involvement in community activities fosters a sense of responsibility and engagement. This involvement can lead to personal growth and a deeper understanding of one's values and passions.

Cultural and Emotional Enrichment

Communities often celebrate cultural and social activities that add richness and joy to life. Participating in community events and cultural celebrations enhances a sense of connection and joy. These events offer you opportunities to learn, share traditions, and create lasting memories. Shared experiences, such as volunteering or attending events, foster emotional bonds and a sense of unity. These collective memories contribute to a deeper sense of joy and fulfillment.

Encouraging Positive Behavior

Being part of a community can encourage positive behavior through social norms and mutual accountability. Communities can promote healthy habits and lifestyles, such as regular exercise, balanced nutrition, and mental well-being practices. Shared endeavors like fitness groups or wellness challenges can make adopting healthy habits more enjoyable and sustainable.

Community involvement often exposes you to new, diverse perspectives and experiences, fostering learning and personal growth. Engaging with different viewpoints and challenges can broaden horizons and deepen understanding. Communities provide a foundation of support that enhances resilience. Knowing that others have your back can boost confidence and the ability to overcome adversity. Communities often pool resources and knowledge, providing members with support and information they might not otherwise have access to. This collective resource sharing enhances individual and community resilience. I wish you luck in your journey of finding the communities that enrich your life and bring joy to you.

The Importance of Giving Back and Its Role in Finding Joy

Paying it forward is a powerful act of kindness, generosity, and compassion that has a profound impact on one's health, mind, and soul. It creates a ripple effect of goodness that extends far beyond the initial act of kindness. When you give to others, you inspire them to do the same, creating a chain reaction of positivity, compassion, and love that uplifts the collective consciousness and nourishes the soul of humanity. Could you volunteer with the school board, a soup kitchen, some type of shelter, or even a city cleanup? There are so many places you can volunteer. Involve your family or friends with you to make more impact. Do something that interests you. Embrace the practice of paying it forward with an open heart and a willingness to make a difference in the lives of others, knowing that by giving generously and authentically, you can create a life that is rich in health, joy, and soulful fulfillment. Giving back, whether through volunteer work, charitable donations, or acts of kindness, plays a vital role in personal fulfillment and joy. The act of contributing to the well-being of others not only benefits recipients but also enriches your life. Here's why giving back is crucial and how it helps you find deeper joy:

Fostering a Sense of Purpose

One of the primary benefits of giving back is the sense of purpose it provides. When we engage in acts of giving, we often find a greater sense of meaning in our daily lives. Knowing that our efforts can make a tangible difference in the lives of others fosters a sense of purpose. Giving back aligns your actions with your personal values and beliefs. This alignment reinforces your identity and life goals, contributing to a more purpose-driven existence. Engaging in acts of generosity has profound effects on your emotional health.

Acts of giving trigger the release of endorphins, natural mood elevators, which can create a *helper's high* and lead to feelings of happiness and satisfaction. Helping others can provide you with a break from your everyday stresses and worries. Focusing on the needs of others shifts attention away from your personal challenges, promoting emotional balance and reducing stress.

Giving back often involves social interaction and collaboration, which strengthen social bonds. Participating in community service or group volunteer activities fosters a sense of belonging and community. These social connections contribute to your overall happiness and a feeling of support. Acts of kindness and generosity can deepen existing relationships. When we help friends, family members, or colleagues, it fosters mutual appreciation and strengthens emotional ties. Giving back nurtures a sense of gratitude and appreciation. Helping those in need provides perspective on personal challenges, often making them seem more manageable. This perspective fosters gratitude for what one has and a deeper appreciation for life's blessings. Engaging in acts of giving highlights the abundance in one's life. Recognizing this abundance fosters a mindset of gratitude and contentment. Giving back encourages personal growth and self-improvement. Acts of giving deepen empathy and compassion. Understanding the struggles and needs of others fosters a more compassionate and kinder demeanor, enriching one's character.

Creating a Positive Legacy

Contributing to the well-being of others helps you build a positive legacy. Acts of giving can create long-lasting positive changes in communities and in individuals' lives. Knowing that your efforts leave a meaningful legacy enhances self-worth and fulfillment. Giving back sets a positive example for others, including children and younger generations. This role modeling encourages a culture of generosity and kindness, amplifying the impact of one's contributions. Overall, giving back contributes to your holistic sense of well-being.

ACTION ITEMS:

What are you doing now for your community?

_____

_____

_____

_____

How can you give back or pay it forward?

_____

_____

_____

_____

List three communities that you would like to explore.
Schedule one in your calendar to visit in the next two weeks.

_____

_____

_____

_____

CALL TO ACTION

Instead of chasing after an idealized version of happiness, I encourage you to focus on life, joy, and love. It is beneficial to shift your focus toward finding joy in the present moment, appreciating small pleasures, and nurturing meaningful connections. By letting go of rigid expectations and embracing the ebb and flow of emotions, you can experience a more genuine and sustainable sense of joy. Filling your life with more joy is a holistic experience that arises from nurturing various aspects of your life. By embracing purpose, gratitude, mindfulness, and resilience, you can cultivate a life filled with joy and fulfillment.

Ultimately, more joy is not found in the absence of difficulties or hardships but in your ability to navigate life's challenges with grace and resilience. By embracing joy in both the highs and lows of life, you can cultivate a more meaningful and lasting sense of fulfillment and contentment. Finding joy in the little things is a powerful practice that can bring happiness and fulfillment to your daily life. Be present in the moment and pay attention to the details around you. Notice the sights, sounds, and sensations that often go unnoticed. By being mindful, you can appreciate the beauty and wonder of the little things. Slow down and savor the experiences you encounter throughout the day. Whether it's enjoying a delicious meal, feeling the warmth of the sun on your skin, or listening to your favorite song, take the time to fully immerse yourself in the moment. Look for beauty in the ordinary moments of life. By appreciating the beauty in everyday things, you can find joy in unexpected places.

Take the time to spread joy to others by performing random acts of kindness. Whether it's offering a smile, lending a helping hand, or giving a thoughtful gift, small gestures of kindness can bring joy to both you and those around you. Take the time to reflect on your day and appreciate the moments of joy you experienced. Write in your journal to capture the little things that brought you happiness. By reflecting and appreciating, you can cultivate a mindset of joy and abundance.

Spread positivity and optimism through your words, actions, and interactions with others. Offer words of encouragement, share uplifting messages, and radiate a sense of hope and possibility that inspires those around you to embrace joy, resilience, and optimism in their lives. By empowering yourself and others to find joy in life, you create a supportive and uplifting environment that fosters personal growth, connection, and well-being. Take it on yourself to create a ripple effect of joy and fulfillment that transforms lives and communities. Embrace the power of joy and positivity as a catalyst for personal and collective growth and watch as the seeds of happiness you plant bloom into a garden of abundance and connection.

Most importantly, developing and coming from a place of love is a life-changing journey that involves cultivating self-love, empathy, kindness, and connection with oneself and others. Love is the oxygen of the human soul. When we operate from a foundation of love, we open ourselves up to deeper relationships, greater fulfillment, and a sense of purpose that transcends individual desires. Live and lead with an open heart. By practicing self-love, cultivating empathy, choosing love over fear, practicing forgiveness, expressing gratitude, being kind, setting boundaries, practicing mindfulness, connecting with nature, and seeking support, you can deepen your capacity to love and be loved. Remember, love is a powerful force that can heal, transform, and uplift both individuals and communities. Embrace the journey of developing and coming from love, and watch as your life becomes a reflection of the boundless power of love and compassion.

Now—not tomorrow or next week— is the time to start creating a joy-filled version of yourself. Immerse your soul in quiet times. Trust your soul. Reignite your light. Focus on what's working and what's not. Get your *why* strong. What change do you need to make to be back on the journey you dreamed of? Get real with yourself. Reset. You are on a new launchpad. Look back over the book and pick three areas to start working on. Record a date on your calendar when you will do a personal check-in to see how those areas are improving. Then pick three more areas to work on going forward in your journey. Be still and throw away all the chatter in our life. Take a clear inventory of your world, health, family, friends, career, and money. What are the areas that need your attention most? It's time to make the changes needed for you to get on the path you desire. You will be humbled by your shortcomings. Expect it. Forgiveness is a major key to moving forward. No more excuses. No more procrastination. Face your fears and slay your dragons. Get your *north star* clear and don't look back. Your decisions will define you, so think with clarity and laser focus your path. Embrace the journey of discovering joy in your life and watch as your days become filled with moments of lightness, laughter, and contentment. Get hungry for what you want in this beautiful life. If you can believe it, see it, and act on it, it will show up.

I wish you a wonderful journey in finding your purpose and passion: Be filled with deep everlasting joy.

Marcia

ABOUT THE AUTHOR

Marcia Fry-Galbraith is a seasoned healthcare professional, keynote speaker, and media consultant with over two decades of experience in the pharmaceutical and biotech industries. As a regional medical director in the pharmaceutical industry, she has led scientific exchanges, developed strategic training programs, and built lasting relationships with industry leaders. Previously, as a medical science liaison, she played a pivotal role in key opinion leader (KOL) engagement, clinical trial site identification, and medical education initiatives.

As a practicing physician assistant in women's health for over twenty-one years, Marcia brings a deep understanding of patient care, healthcare policy, and effective communication. She has also served as the director of patient services at Planned Parenthood of Orange County (California) and CEO of a medical education company, further expanding her expertise in advocacy and education.

Beyond her corporate and clinical experience, Marcia is a nationally recognized speaker and consultant, having appeared on ABC, CBS, NBC, and PBS, as well as over one hundred radio stations. Her ability to translate complex medical concepts into engaging, accessible content has made her a sought-after trainer, coach, and thought leader in the healthcare industry.

Now, she brings her passion for education and connection to the world of publishing. Through her signature blend of expertise, storytelling, and insight, she empowers readers to embrace joy as an essential part of their personal and professional journeys.

For more information, you can contact Marcia at **marciafrygalbraith.com** or scan the QR code above.

ENDNOTES

i American Psychological Association, "Stress in America 2023: A Nation Recovering from Collective Trauma," American Psychological Association, November 2023, https://www.apa.org/news/press/releases/stress/2023/collective-trauma-recovery

ii *APA Dictionary of Psychology*, "resilience," last updated April 19, 2018, https://dictionary.apa.org/resilience.

iii Micah Abraham, "Anxiety and Negative Thoughts," CalmClinic, February 9, 2022, https://www.calmclinic.com/anxiety/symptoms/bad-thoughts.

iv Melissa G. Hunt, Rachel Marx, Courtney Lipson, and Jordyn Young, "No More FOMO: Limiting Social Media Decreases Loneliness and Depression," *Journal of Social and Clinical Psychology*, *37*, no. 10 (2018): 751–768, https://doi.org/10.1521/jscp.2018.37.10.751.

v Ann Rousseau and Rachel F. Rodgers, "Social Media Incidental Exposure and Young People's Body Image: A Conceptual Review," *Body Image* 52, (2025): 11838, https://doi.org/10.1016/j.bodyim.2024.101838.

vi Sakshi Prasad, Sara Ait Souabni, Gibson Anugwom, et al., "Anxiety and Depression Amongst Youth as Adverse Effects of Using Social Media: A Review," *Annals of Medicine & Surgery* 85, no. 8 (2023): 3974–3981, https://doi.org/10.1097/MS9.0000000000001066.

vii Samantha Kemp, "It's a Mean, Mean World: Social Media and Mean World Syndrome" (university honors thesis, Portland State University, 2023), https://doi.org/10.15760/honors.1333.

viii Polly Campbell, "Excessive News Consumption May Harm Mental and Physical Health: Break the News Cycle Before It Breaks You," *Psychology Today*, September 27, 2022, https://www. psychologytoday.com/us/blog/imperfect-spirituality/202209/ excessive-news-consumption-may-harm-mental-and-physical-health.

ix Gallup, *State of the Global Workplace: 2024 Report* (Gallup Inc., 2024), https:// www.gallup.com/workplace/349484/state-of-the-global-workplace.aspx.

x Julianne Holt-Lunstad, Timothy B. Smith, and J. Bradley Layton, "Social Relationships and Mortality Risk: A Meta-Analytic Review," *PLoS Med* 7, no. 7 (2010): e1000316, https://doi.org/10.1371/journal.pmed.1000316.

xi Gulia Cambieri, "The Importance of Connections: Ways to Live a Longer, Healthier Life," Harvard T. H. Chan School of Public Health, last modified December 16, 2024, https://hsph.harvard.edu/news/ the-importance-of-connections-ways-to-live-a-longer-healthier-life/.

xii "Exercise and Stress: Get Moving to Manage Stress," Healthy Lifestyle and Stress Management, Mayo Clinic, August 3, 2022, https://www.mayoclinic.org/ healthy-lifestyle/stress-management/in-depth/exercise-and-stress/art-20044469.

xiii Emma Childs and Hariet de Wit, "Regular Exercise Is Associated with Emotional Resilience to Acute Stress in Healthy Adults," *Frontiers in Physiology* 5 (2014): 161, https://doi.org/10.3389/fphys.2014.00161.

xiv Thorsten Barnhofer, Catherine Crane, Emily Hargus, Myanthi Amarasinghe, Rosie Winder, and J. Mark G. Williams, "Mindfulness-Based Cognitive Therapy as a Treatment for Chronic Depression: A Preliminary Study," *Behaviour Research and Therapy* 47, no. 5 (2009): 366–373, https://doi.org/10.1016/j. brat.2009.01.019.

xv Juliana Breines, "Four Great Gratitude Strategies," *Greater Good Magazine*, June 30, 2015, https://greatergood.berkeley.edu/article/item/ four_great_gratitude_strategies.

xvi Andrea Gragnano, Silvia Simbula, and Massimo Miglioretti, "Work-Life Balance: Weighing the Importance of Work-Family and Work-Health Balance," *International Journal of Environmental Research and Public Health* 17, no. 3 (2020): 907, https://doi.org/10.3390/ijerph17030907.

xvii Jingping Xu and Robert E. Roberts, "The Power of Positive Emotions: It's a Matter of Life or Death—Subjective Well-Being and Longevity over 28 Years in a General Population," *Health Psychology* 29, no. 1 (2010): 9–19, https://doi.org/10.1037/a0016767.

xviii Liz Mineo, "Harvard Study, Almost 80 Years Old, Has Proved that Embracing Community Helps Us Live Longer, and Be Happier," *The Harvard Gazette*, April 11, 2017, https://news.harvard.edu/gazette/story/2017/04/over-nearly-80-years-harvard-study-has-been-showing-how-to-live-a-healthy-and-happy-life/.

xix Shilpa Thakur, "The Impact of Food Quality on Weight Management and Energy Regulation!," LinkedIn, November 1, 2024, https://www.linkedin.com/pulse/impact-food-quality-weight-management-energy-medical-nutrition-ufduc/.

xx Natlie Terry and Kara Gross Margolis, "Seratonergic Mechanisms Regulating the GI Tract: Experimental evidence and Therapeutic Relevance," in *Handbook of Experimental Pharmacology*, ed. J. E. Barrett, vol. 239, *Gastrointestinal Pharmacology*, ed. Beverley Greenwood-Van Meerveld (Springer, 2017) 319–342, https://doi.org/10.1007/164_2016_103.

xxi Terry and Margolis, "Seratonergic Mechanisms."

xxii G. B. Rogers, D. J. Keating, R. L. Young, M. L. Wong, J. Licinio, and S. Wesselingh, "From Gut Dysbiosis to Altered Brain Function and Mental Illness: Mechanisms and Pathways," *Molecular Psychiatry* 21 (2016): 738–748, https://doi.org/10.1038/mp.2016.50.

xxiii Jane E. Brody, "A Positive Outlook May Be Good for Your Health," *The New York Times*, March 17, 2017, https://www.nytimes.com/2017/03/27/well/live/positive-thinking-may-improve-health-and-extend-life.html.